Sport Fish
of Florida

FS Books:

Sportsman's Best: Inshore Fishing
Sportsman's Best: Trout
Sportsman's Best: Redfish
Sportsman's Best: Snapper & Grouper
Sportsman's Best: Offshore Fishing
Sportsman's Best: Sailfish
Sportsman's Best: Dolphin

Sport Fish of Florida
Sport Fish of the Gulf of Mexico
Sport Fish of the Atlantic
Sport Fish of Fresh Water
Sport Fish of the Pacific

Baits, Rigs & Tackle
Annual Fishing Planner
The Angler's Cookbook

Florida Sportsman Magazine
Shallow Water Angler Magazine
Florida Sportsman Fishing Charts
Lawsticks
Law Boatstickers

Edited by Eric Wickstrom
Art Director by Drew Wickstrom
Copy Edited by Jerry McBride

www.floridasportsman.com

Sport Fish
of Florida

By Vic Dunaway

Original Illustrations by
Kevin R. Brant

www.floridasportsman.com

CONTENTS

SECTION 2
Fresh Water

Preface

What's That on My Line?

"What's the name of this fish anyway?"

"Is it good to eat?"

Those are two big questions that many thousands of fishermen constantly ask as they encounter the huge variety of fish in Florida's inshore and offshore waters.

Until now, there has been no complete, easy-to-use identification guide. *Sport Fish of Florida* fills that need. All the fish you're likely to catch are shown on these pages. Well over 200 of them. No more guesswork.

I. D. information, edibility ratings and other important information are provided by none other than Vic Dunaway, founding editor of *Florida Sportsman Magazine*. A legend, who really is just that, Vic knows his sport fish like no one else.

Sport Fish of Florida also features all original illustrations by Floridian Kevin R. Brant, who carefully produced the images exclusively for this long-awaited book.

At *Florida Sportsman*, we've talked periodically for 20 years about the need for a really helpful guidebook that would show all the key fish and give the salient facts about them for the typical angler. Lo and behold, here it is!

We trust that you'll find *Sport Fish of Florida* to be a helpful companion for your angling days in state and neighboring waters, where the fish are both diverse and delectable.

—*Karl Wickstrom, Publisher*
Florida Sportsman Magazine

The Angler's Practical Guide

The good, the bad, the ugly—for the very first time, they're all here together in a book of their own, a book that illustrates and describes virtually every kind of fish an angler in Florida—or the Bahamas or Caribbean Islands—could expect to find on the end of a line.

In this book you'll find the scoop on every hook-and-line species from the mightiest Marlin to the lowliest Lizardfish, along with advice on how to catch each one and how good it is to eat.

Because it's designed as a practical guide for fishermen, every effort has been made to keep biological jargon at bay. However, there is one nod to the world of science that is unavoidable—the inclusion of scientific names so that each of the species can be definitely pinpointed. Without scientific names, confusion would reign, because most species are known by more than one common name and, in many cases, two or more different species share the same common name.

It would have been nice to sort the species by their preferred environment—offshore, inshore, reef, flats or whatever. But, as fishermen realize all too well, fish have tails and can swim where they please. The same kind of fish you catch on a flat today and in a bridge channel tomorrow may well strike your bait out on the deep reef next weekend. The constant element of surprise is one of the most appealing aspects of angling in this great area.

Alphabetical and strictly scientific classifications would have other drawbacks, so it was decided to use a mixed system that lets the species fall into whatever groupings would be natural. Most of the chapters cover a particular family of fishes. Some, however, deal with species that are not related but have certain habits or attributes in common. All are listed in a complete index at the end of the book.

BE SURE TO ABIDE BY THE LAW

A great many kinds of fish are protected by conservation laws that may include licenses, daily bag limits, possession limits, minimum and maximum size limits, permitting and other legal requirements. Many different jurisdictions and agencies are involved in managing the fisheries—at least a half-dozen in Florida alone, to say nothing of other countries—and their regulations sometimes conflict.

In Florida, information is available from such sources as *Florida Sportsman Magazine*, county courthouses and many tackle shops. Visitors to Florida or the Islands usually are able to get the needed information from their travel agents, resorts, fishing camps or charter captains.

BEWARE OF TOXIC FISH

Ciguatera is a type of poison carried by certain individual fish in tropical waters. Although only a minute number of fish are affected, people sometimes acquire the toxin, mostly by eating very big specimens of predatory types, such as the Great Barracuda, Amberjack, and even some larger varieties of Grouper and Snapper. The resulting illness can be serious and lingering, but is rarely fatal.

Ciguatera seems to be more common in some species than in others, but its occurrence is rarely predictable. In a given area, a few fish of a particular species may be carriers of the toxin while the majority of individuals of that same species are perfectly safe to eat.

The toxin comes from microscopic organisms called dinoflagellates that attach themselves to marine algae. Grazing fishes acquire the toxin by eating the algae. Predators acquire it by eating the grazers; however, it must accumulate in the muscle tissue of the predator for a considerable amount of time before reaching levels that are dangerous to human beings. It is always wise to let the big predators go and eat the smaller ones.

A second kind of marine fish illness—Puffer poisoning—is more serious—often fatal, in fact. But it is also far more easily avoided. All you have to do is refrain from eating any of the Puffers.

In fresh water, the roe of Gars is also known to be poisonous.

Fortunately, toxic fish are relatively rare. Our waters offer a tremendous variety of delicious species for all to enjoy.

Inside Your Sport Fish Book

The presentation for each species is headed by an illustration, along with its most often used common name and its scientific name. Then come the following sub-headed paragraphs:

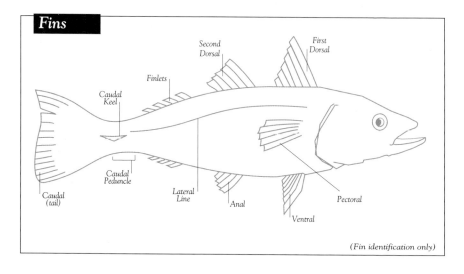

Fins

Second Dorsal

First Dorsal

Finlets

Caudal Keel

Caudal Peduncle

Caudal (tail)

Lateral Line

Anal

Ventral

Pectoral

(Fin identification only)

DESCRIPTION: Color and markings alone aren't always reliable guides to fish identification, so this paragraph provides the reader with identifiable features that, in combination with the illustration, should serve to make identification positive. It does not go into the counting of scale rows, gill rakers or other anatomic details that very few anglers can muster the patience it takes to stop and investigate. In the majority of cases, however, the fins provide obvious clues and are often referred to in the description.

SIZE: Chief concern here is to give the angler an idea of the size, or range of sizes, that are commonly encountered, but mention is made of approximate maximum sizes as well. The absolute size potential is not known for any species, of course—which is why world records keep rising.

FOOD VALUE: Offers a guide as to how good the fish is to eat. But you should take note that, with only a handful of exceptions, all fish are edible and most of them are more than acceptable. Any relative rating of table quality is bound to be highly subjective.

GAME QUALITIES: Describes—again in the author's opinion—the merits and characteristics of the fight the species usually puts up on the end of a line.

OTHER NAMES:

Lists any other popular name, or names, known to be in use. The same common or alternate names may, at times, be given for more than one fish.

RANGE: Here, note is made of the usual range of the particular species within the book's covered area only—not the complete range, which may be far wider. The areas covered are Florida, the Bahamas and the Caribbean Islands. The larger islands of the Caribbean comprise the Greater Antilles—Cuba, Jamaica, Hispaniola (Haiti and the

TACKLE AND BAITS: Lists the most suitable kind and weight of fishing gear for the particular species, along with examples of the best baits and lures.

FISHING SYSTEMS: Lists the best or most used approaches to fishing for the particular fish under the following categories: Still Fishing (fishing with natural bait from an anchored boat, or from bridge, pier or land); Trolling (pulling baits or lures behind a boat under manual or mechanical power); Drift Fishing (trailing baits behind a boat moved only by wind or current); and Casting. You could, of course, cast artificial lures in any of the other listed situations, but as a separate category it denotes moving about and casting lures or flies, either to sighted fish or to selected target areas, whether the moving about is done on foot or from a boat propelled by pole, paddle or slow motor.

Dominican Republic) and Puerto Rico. All the rest make up the Lesser Antilles. Because they offer considerable freshwater estuarine habitat, the Greater Antilles are home to many coastal fishes that occur in Florida but may not be found to any great extent in the Bahamas or smaller islands of the Caribbean.

HABITAT: Outlines the type or types of environment in which the angler is most likely to hook up with the subject species.

Despite the unglamorous name, the Croaker family encompasses many of Florida's most popular game and food fish, including the two that would head any list of statewide inshore favorites—the Spotted Seatrout and the Redfish. Moreover, all these fish are cooperative strikers, good gamesters and tasty table fare. And most of them are routinely caught by shorebound anglers as well as boaters. None of the fish covered in this section are common in the Bahamas or Caribbean Islands.

The Croakers

Spotted Seatrout

Weakfish

Sand Seatrout

Silver Seatrout

Red Drum

Black Drum

Atlantic Croaker

Silver Perch

Spot

Northern Kingfish

Southern Kingfish

Gulf Kingfish

Spotted Seatrout

Cynoscion nebulosus

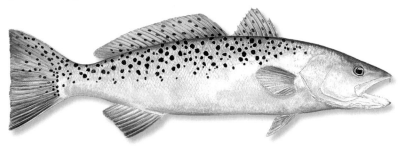

OTHER NAMES:

Trout
Speckled Trout
Speck

RANGE: *All Florida coasts.*

HABITAT: *Spotted Seatrout can be caught in virtually any of Florida's inshore waters, from the outside surf to far up coastal rivers, and, at times, in fairly deep Gulf water. Most commonly caught from spring through fall on shallow grassy flats and in grass-lined channels and holes. During cold snaps, they run far up coastal rivers.*

DESCRIPTION: Streamlined shape; large mouth with prominent canine teeth; color gray or silvery with many prominent black spots on sides. Background may be quite dark, or gold, when fish are in back bays or streams.

SIZE: Usually 1-2 pounds; common on both coasts to about four pounds. Largest fish, both in average size and maximum size, come from East-Central region, where fish to 10 pounds are taken at times and where potential is to 15 pounds or more. Gulf Coast trout are considered large at 5-8 pounds, but can top 10. World and Florida records 17 pounds, 7 ounces.

FOOD VALUE: A table favorite.

GAME QUALITIES: Not exceedingly strong or active, but a hard striker on a variety of baits and quite sporty on light gear. Showy, surface-thrashing fighter but not a long runner. Sometimes jumps.

TACKLE AND BAITS: Spinning, baitcasting and fly tackle are all effective and sporting. Best natural baits are live shrimp, live baitfish and strips of cut Mullet or Pinfish. Most popular lures are bait-tail jigs, swimming plugs and topwater plugs. Poppers are productive fly-rod lures over the flats; large streamers work in all waters.

FISHING SYSTEMS: Drifting; Still Fishing; Casting.

Weakfish

Cynoscion regalis

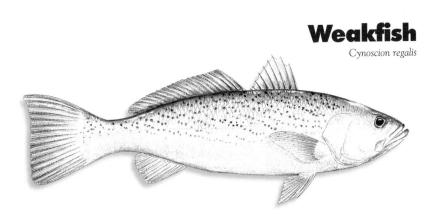

DESCRIPTION: Silhouette similar to the spotted seatrout, but markings take the form of irregular wavy lines instead of spots. Prominent canine teeth.

SIZE: Average is 1-3 pounds. Does not grow as large in Florida as in northeastern states, although fish over 5 pounds are possible. World record 19 pounds, 2 ounces; Florida record 10 pounds.

FOOD VALUE: Very good.

GAME QUALITIES: Less of a surface brawler than the Speckled Trout, but gives a good account of itself on light gear.

TACKLE AND BAITS: Spinning and baitcasting; fly fishing usually difficult. Weakfish bite best on live shrimp, but will take live baitfish and strips of fish. Best lures are jigs, worked slow and deep.

FISHING SYSTEMS: Still Fishing; Drifting; Casting.

OTHER NAMES:
Gray Trout
Northern Trout

RANGE: *From North Florida, south to Cape Canaveral; stragglers perhaps to Fort Pierce on the East Coast.*

HABITAT: *Most fishing for Weakfish takes place in the Jacksonville area and Port Canaveral. This species prefers deeper water, as a rule, than its spotted cousin; channels, deep holes, basins and harbors.*

Sand Seatrout "White Trout"

Cynoscion arenarius

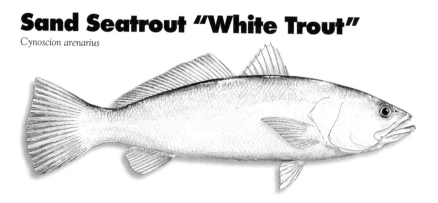

OTHER NAMES:

Sand Trout

RANGE: *All Florida coasts.*

HABITAT: *Most are caught in deep portions of bays and channels on the Gulf Coast, but are present on the Atlantic side as well. Generally prefers hard sand or shell bottom, but sometimes mixes with Speckled Trout on grass flats.*

DESCRIPTION: Often confused with the Silver Trout (see next), and both can be confused with the Weakfish (previous) but note that, with rare exception, the Weakfish is found in the Atlantic and both the others in the Gulf. This fish is tan or yellowish above and silver below. No spots. Canine teeth present.

SIZE: Usually one-half to one pound; rarely exceeds 2. World record 6 pounds, 2 ounces.

FOOD VALUE: Smaller ones with skin on are tasty panfish. Those over a pound or so produce mild-flavored fillets.

GAME QUALITIES: Short runs. Fun, but no challenge.

TACKLE AND BAITS: Light spinning tackle is best. Favored baits are shrimp, live or dead, and small strips of fish or squid. Small leadhead jigs are tops as artificials.

FISHING SYSTEMS: Still Fishing; Drifting; Casting.

Silver Seatrout

Cynoscion nothus

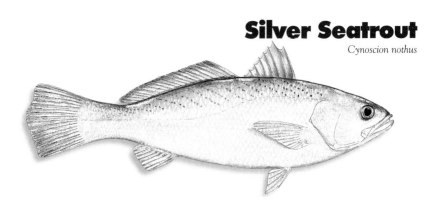

DESCRIPTION: Similar in appearance to, and often confused with, the White Trout (preceding), but is smaller and of a decidedly more silvery hue overall.

SIZE: Average is 6 to 10 inches; an occasional fish may reach or slightly exceed one pound.
World record 1 pound, 2 ounces.

FOOD VALUE: A fine panfish, but seldom large enough to make filleting worthwhile. Best prepared by scaling and drawing, then pan-frying.

GAME QUALITIES: Generally too small to put up much resistance, but can put a bend in a light spinning rod when being hauled up from deep water.

TACKLE AND BAITS: Light spinning tackle with small hooks and pieces of shrimp or cut fish. Willingly hit leadhead jigs. A tandem rig works very well—made by using a very small jig as a trailer behind a larger one that sinks faster. Combine the two by tying a foot of light monofilament line to the eye of the front jig, then tying the eye of the smaller jig to the other end.

FISHING SYSTEMS: Still Fishing; Drifting.

OTHER NAMES:
Silver Trout

RANGE: All Florida coasts, but more plentiful in the upper half of the state.

HABITAT: Basically, this is a fish of open water, but most of them are caught by Florida anglers during colder seasons, when they invade the deep channels of harbors and bays.

Red Drum "Redfish"
Sciaenops ocellatus

OTHER NAMES:
Red Bass
Channel Bass
Drum

RANGE: All Florida coasts.

HABITAT: Most popular fishing areas are along shell bars and rocky or grassy shorelines and on shallow flats, where they are usually fished by sight. Reds also forage in the surf of outside beaches nearly everywhere on the Gulf Coast and along the upper half of the East Coast, especially in the fall. Adults move offshore to spawn and are sometimes encountered in open water in large schools. They roam into coastal rivers and creeks at any time of year, and in winter swarm into them, seeking warmer water.

DESCRIPTION: Usually bronze or reddish with white underside, but sometimes quite pale all over. Prominent ringed spot or several spots at base of tail fin; occasionally, without the spot. Silhouette is similar to black drum and colors can sometimes be confusing in very large fish, but the redfish has no chin barbels and the black drum never has the tail spot.

SIZE: Caught from less than a pound to 10 or 12 pounds; 30-pounders are not rare, and the potential in Florida is about 60. World record 94 pounds, 2 ounces; Florida record 52 pounds, 5 ounces.

FOOD VALUE: Redfish up to around 10 pounds rank among the favorite fish of most anglers. Red portions of flesh do not have objectionable taste when fresh. Large Redfish are protected at this writing, and not the best of fare anyway.

GAME QUALITIES: Fine gamester. Strength, stamina and fairly long, bullish runs are its trademarks.

TACKLE AND BAITS: All kinds of casting tackle, including fly, are successfully used on Redfish of all sizes. Surf rods and light-to-medium saltwater outfits are good for beach, bridge, pier and offshore fishing. Redfish are ravenous feeders that will take live baitfish, crabs and shrimp, and also dead or cut baits from the same sources. Live shrimp and minnows make the very best baits for shallow coastal fishing; live Pinfish, small Mullet or similar baitfish for angling in deeper water. Most productive artificials are weedless spoons, plastic-tail jigs and topwater plugs, but many swimming plugs also work. Large streamers and poppers do the job for fly fishermen.

FISHING SYSTEMS: Still Fishing; Drifting; Casting.

Black Drum

Pogonias cromis

DESCRIPTION: Somewhat similar to the Redfish in shape, but usually distinguishable by color, and always by the fact that the Drum has barbels, or feelers on the underside of the lower jaw. Juvenile Drum have black vertical stripes on dusky white sides, as do Sheepshead (which see). Only novices will be confused, however, because Drum lack the prominent sheep-like teeth that give the Sheepshead its name. The stripes fade with age and adult Drum are usually blackish above and white below, although some develop a decidedly bronze hue.

SIZE: Drum over 100 pounds have been caught and specimens weighing 30 to 50 pounds are not rare in many areas. Striped juveniles generally weigh 1-15 pounds. World record 113 pounds, 1 ounce; Florida record 96 pounds.

FOOD VALUE: Drum to about 6 or 8 pounds are as tasty as Redfish. Larger ones become quite coarse.

GAME QUALITIES: Strong, bullish fight, but not so tough as the Redfish, size for size.

TACKLE AND BAITS: Surf tackle and saltwater boat rods are used when targeting big fish, but even the lunkers can be caught rather easily on spinning and casting tackle with a bit of patience. Fly fishing is a challenge. Any sort of crustacean, from shrimp to cut blue crab to whole small crab, makes fine bait for Drum. Cut fish and squid work fairly well. Drum are not avid lure-chasers but can be taken on slowly worked jigs in deep water, and by carefully presented streamer flies and jigs on the flats.

FISHING SYSTEMS: Still Fishing; Casting.

OTHER NAMES:

Drum

Striped Drum

RANGE: *All Florida coasts.*

HABITAT: *Surf and estuarine areas. Most consistently productive fisheries for big Drum are found in the St. Marys River estuary of the northeast coast, the Indian River, Tampa Bay and the Suwannee River estuary. Like Redfish, small Drum forage along shell bars, shorelines and on shallow flats. Big fish stick mostly to inside channels and surf.*

Atlantic Croaker
Micropogonias undulatus

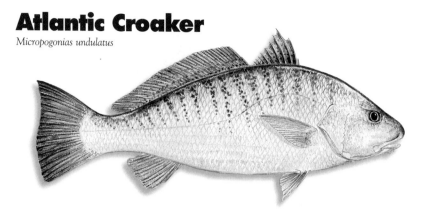

OTHER NAMES:

Croaker

Hardhead

RANGE: *Occurs statewide but is more common in the upper half of Florida.*

HABITAT: *Likes sand or shell bottom. It's a regular catch in many surf areas but also can be caught from sloughs and channels of inside waters, particularly those with soft bottom.*

DESCRIPTION: Similar to the Black Drum in outline, but a much smaller fish. Overall silvery or gold background with sometimes indistinct wavy lines on upper sides. Like the Black Drum, it has small barbels on underside of lower jaw.

SIZE: Averages a pound or less, but sometimes reaches 3 pounds, or perhaps slightly more. World and Florida records 5 pounds, 8 ounces.

FOOD VALUE: Small ones make good panfish; some are large enough to provide fillets. Either way, the flesh is of a mild flavor.

GAME QUALITIES: Scrappy on very light tackle but, unfortunately, many are taken on heavy surf gear. Against a light line, they run fairly well and can also use the waves to good advantage in the surf.

TACKLE AND BAITS: Light spinning or baitcasting; light surf outfits. Top baits include live and dead shrimp, sand fleas, fiddler crabs, cut squid, cut fish. Croakers will also take small jigs. The combination of a little jig with a bit of shrimp on the hook is deadly.

FISHING SYSTEMS: Still Fishing.

Silver Perch

Bairdiella chrysoura

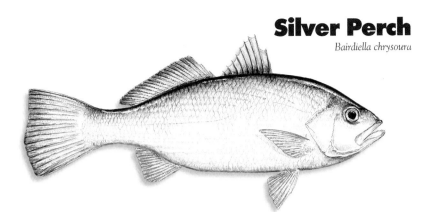

DESCRIPTION: Grayish or steel back, silvery on sides. Fins and tail yellowish. Confused in name and appearance with the Silver Trout (which see), but this is not a Seatrout, although related. Absence of canine teeth is the giveaway.

SIZE: Up to perhaps 10 inches; common at 4-6 inches.

FOOD VALUE: An excellent panfish; seldom large enough to fillet. Rolled in meal and deep-fried, they are delicious.

GAME QUALITIES: Too small to provide much sport, but they at least provide some action on many winter days when the sought-after Redfish and Trout are hard to find.

TACKLE AND BAITS: Light spinning tackle with small hooks and pieces of shrimp, fish or squid. They readily hit artificials and are easily hooked on very small jigs.

FISHING SYSTEMS: Still Fishing; Casting.

OTHER NAMES:
Yellowtail
Sugar Trout
Silver Trout

RANGE: Inshore waters, mostly in the upper half of Florida. Seems to be more plentiful on the Gulf Coast, especially the Panhandle and Big Bend areas.

HABITAT: Abundant in coastal rivers and streams during the winter—sometimes schooling so thickly that catches could be made by the dozens, or even hundreds, if an angler were so inclined.

Spot

Leiostomus xanthurus

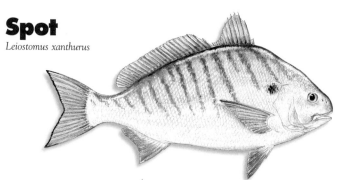

OTHER NAMES:
Spotted Croaker
Mizzouki Croaker

RANGE: *Common on Atlantic Coast, except south of Palm Beach County. Also found in lesser numbers along most of the Gulf Coast.*

HABITAT: *Very common in the surf; also bays and inlets.*

DESCRIPTION: Easily distinguished from other Croakers and similar panfish by its forked tail and prominent spot behind the gill cover. Brassy color with wavy or mottled lines above; fading to white on underside. World record 1 pound.

SIZE: Averages 6-8 inches; rarely reaches one pound.

FOOD VALUE: One of the most popular panfish.

GAME QUALITIES: Spirited panfish.

TACKLE AND BAITS: Light spinning tackle, small hooks, pieces of cut fish, squid or shrimp.

FISHING SYSTEMS: Still Fishing.

Northern Kingfish

Menticirrhus saxatilis

OTHER NAMES:
Northern Whiting

RANGE: *All Florida coasts.*

HABITAT: *Surf, channels, passes, inlets and sand bars.*

DESCRIPTION: Dark bars are more vivid than on the Southern Kingfish.

SIZE: Under 1 pound as a rule; sometimes 2 pounds. World record 2 pounds, 7 ounces.

FOOD VALUE: Good.

GAME QUALITIES: Scrappy on light tackle.

TACKLE AND BAITS: See Southern Kingfish.

FISHING SYSTEMS: Still Fishing.

Southern Kingfish
Menticirrhus americanus

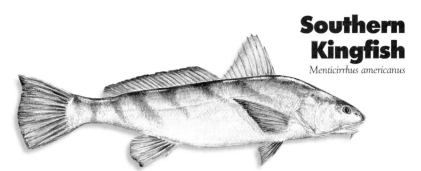

DESCRIPTION: Large head with one barbel at tip of lower jaw. Flattened belly. Overall silvery color, tannish on top. Indistinct dark blotches on side.

SIZE: Usually less than a pound. Sometimes 2 pounds. World record 2 pounds, 13 ounces.

FOOD VALUE: Bland but good.

GAME QUALITIES: Runs well against very light tackle.

TACKLE AND BAITS: Light spinning, casting and surf tackle. Best baits are sand fleas and pieces of shrimp or squid. Readily hits small jigs and flies. On bright, calm days, Whiting can be sight-fished at the very edge of the surf along many beaches.

FISHING SYSTEMS: Still Fishing; Casting.

OTHER NAMES:
Southern Whiting
King Whiting

RANGE: All Florida coasts; more common in Atlantic.

HABITAT: Roams sandy bottom. Abundant surf fish.

Gulf Kingfish
Menticirrhus littoralis

DESCRIPTION: Body shape same as Southern Kingfish, but is silvery all over with no pattern on sides. Tail black-tipped.

SIZE: Under 1 pound as a rule; sometimes 2 pounds.

FOOD VALUE: Good.

GAME QUALITIES: Scrappy on light tackle.

TACKLE AND BAITS: See Southern Kingfish.

FISHING SYSTEMS: Still Fishing; Casting.

OTHER NAMES:
Gulf Whiting

RANGE: This is the common Whiting of the Gulf Coast, but occurs on Atlantic side as well.

HABITAT: Surf, channels, passes, inlets and sand bars.

Many anglers are surprised when they learn that four distinct species of Snook can be found in the South Atlantic and parts of the Caribbean. Three of them, however, must be ranked mostly as curiosities, since they are seldom caught and even more rarely kept. Florida law imposes a minimum legal size for Snook and it's unlikely that two of the "odd three" species could even conceivably reach it.

Of course, the main species is Snook enough anyway, having been ranked, according to several surveys, as the species most Florida anglers would prefer to catch if they had any choice in the matter. Snook are fixtures in the Greater Antilles but rarities in most of the other islands.

The Snooks

Common Snook

Fat Snook

Swordspine Snook

Tarpon Snook

Common Snook

Centropomus undecimalis

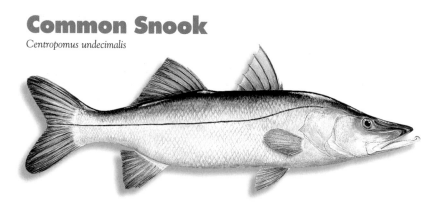

OTHER NAMES:
Lineside
Robalo
Ravillia

RANGE: *A tropical species, Snook are found on the larger islands of the Caribbean, including Cuba, Puerto Rico and Hispaniola. They are absent from the Bahamas, except for an occasional straggler in Bimini. In Florida, they are largely confined to about the lower half of the Peninsula. However, a few successive years without damaging freezes will send them spreading northward, particularly on the Atlantic Coast, where they have been fishable even around Jacksonville at times. On the Gulf side, the Homosassa River seems to be the limit of their range, although wandering individuals are caught in the Panhandle on occasion. Even on the lower Gulf Coast, occasional freezes kill many Snook. Serious kills are far less common on the Atlantic side, where deeper, warmer water is closer at hand to provide a haven.*

DESCRIPTION: The Snook has a most distinctive body shape, featuring a tapered head and snout, underslung lower jaw, large fins and, most distinctive of all, a prominent black stripe running the full length of the lateral line. The stripe is present in all species of Snook. Coloration is generally dark gray to black on the dorsal surface, shading to silvery on the sides. The fins are yellowish. As with many inshore fish, the coloration may vary with season and habitat. Snook of inside waters usually have darker sides.

SIZE: Generally, the size range is from 3 to 15 pounds. Snook weighing 20 to 30 pounds are not unusual on either coast, especially around inlets and passes during the summer, when spawning takes place. A number of Snook topping 40 pounds have been caught over the years on both coasts, and the maximum may be 60 or more. World record 53 pounds, 10 ounces; Florida record 44 pounds, 3 ounces

FOOD VALUE: Snook are proportionately very thick through the shoulders, and their fillets represent a higher portion of total weight than most other fish. The fillets are mild yet flavorful and are ranked at the top of nearly everyone's list of favorite fish.

GAME QUALITIES: One of the best for all-around fighting ability. The fight is usually featured by several long runs and a few jumps. Small Snook leap high in the manner of Ladyfish, while the really big females manage to clear only about half their bodies. Snook also are past masters at utilizing shoreline roots or any other obstructions to their advantage.

TACKLE AND BAITS: Even though spinning and baitcasting tackle are the most used, light saltwater boat rods get plenty of action, particularly when live-baiting in passes and inlets. Even heavier gear often gets the call for fishing from piers and bridges. Surf tackle can be useful at times, although surf Snook are usually close to the beach, in easy range of casting gear. Fly fishermen take their Snook on large streamers and poppers, for the most part, while hard-lure casters rely heavily on mirror plugs, bucktail and plastic jigs, jerk plugs, spoons and topwater plugs. Any small fish makes good live bait, as do live shrimp and crabs. Schooling baitfish, such as Pilchards, work wonders as both live chum and bait. Large dead baits fished on bottom take some very big Snook; best are Mullet heads and Ladyfish heads or halves.

FISHING SYSTEMS: Still Fishing; Casting; Trolling; Drift Fishing.

HABITAT: *Snook are fished in a variety of settings—mangrove shorelines; grassy flats and potholes; passes and inlets. They love to hang around bridge and pier pilings, or any kind of snag. They also are excellent surf fish in many areas.*

Fat Snook
Centropomus parallelus

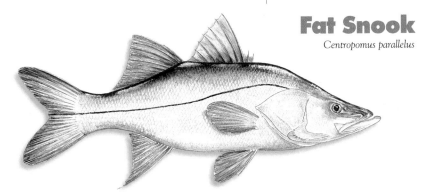

DESCRIPTION: Shorter and deeper in silhouette than the Common Snook.

SIZE: The Fat Snook is probably the only one of the three lesser species that occasionally exceeds 20 inches in length. May reach 24 inches, although most are 12-16 inches long. World Record 10 pounds, 14 ounces.

FOOD VALUE: Excellent but seldom tried.

GAME QUALITIES: Good jumper and strong for its size.

TACKLE AND BAITS: The lightest spinning, baitcasting and fly tackle, with small jigs, surface and swimming plugs; also streamer flies and popping bugs. Good natural baits are live shrimp, Pilchards, small Pinfish.

FISHING SYSTEMS: Still Fishing; Casting; Trolling.

OTHER NAMES:
**Cuban Snook
Calba**

RANGE: *In Florida, south of Lake Okeechobee. Not common anywhere, but not too unusual in Dade and Broward Counties, and the Keys. Occurs also on larger islands of the Caribbean.*

HABITAT: *Likes mangroves; small canals and streams.*

Swordspine Snook

Centropomus ensiferus

OTHER NAMES:

Little Snook

RANGE: *The Swordspine is also the rarest of Florida's Snook species, probably occurring only in protected canals and streams of extreme South Florida. It also is found in the Caribbean.*

HABITAT: *Most have been reported from freshwater ponds and canals from the Upper Keys to St. Lucie County on the East Coast, and the 10,000 Islands of the Gulf Coast.*

DESCRIPTION: The long, sharp spine of the anal fin, when folded against the body, extends past the beginning of the caudal (tail) fin. Other species of Snook have similarly impressive anal fin spines, but not so long.

SIZE: The smallest snook; a foot or so at most. World record 1 pound, 9 ounces.

FOOD VALUE: Not eaten because of size, but fine.

GAME QUALITIES: The Swordspine strikes voraciously and gives as good a show as it can for its modest heft.

TACKLE AND BAITS: The lightest spinning, baitcasting and fly tackle with small jigs and flies; live shrimp.

FISHING SYSTEMS: Still Fishing; Casting.

Tarpon Snook

Centropomus pectinatus

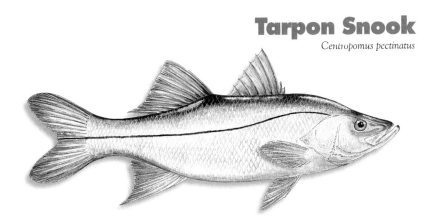

DESCRIPTION: The name refers to the upturned forward portion of the head, which somewhat resembles that of the Tarpon. The body is much more compressed than in other species.

SIZE: May reach 20 inches; usual maximum is 15 inches. World record 3 pounds, 2 ounces.

FOOD VALUE: Good but usually not eaten.

GAME QUALITIES: A good battler for its size, but its slighter body makes it less sporty than similar sizes of Common and Fat Snook.

TACKLE AND BAITS: The lightest spinning, baitcasting and fly tackle, with small jigs, surface and swimming plugs, streamer flies. Preferred naturals are live shrimp, Pilchards, small Pinfish.

FISHING SYSTEMS: Still Fishing; Casting; Trolling.

RANGE: Large Caribbean Islands, plus Dade, Broward and Palm Beach Counties and the Keys; also reported from the lower Gulf Coast to Fort Myers.

HABITAT: Mangrove areas, canals. Like the Common Snook, hangs around bridge and dock pilings.

A number of different flatfish occur in Florida, but only three are both common enough and large enough to be of significant interest to anglers. Perhaps it is only two, because not everyone believes that the Summer Flounder (Fluke) occurs in Florida at all. If it does, it is restricted to the northernmost Atlantic Coast of the state and even there would be far less numerous than the similar Southern Flounder. All of these are "left-eyed" Flounders, meaning that, when viewed from above and with the dorsal fin on top, the eyes are on the left.

The Flounders

Southern Flounder

Gulf Flounder

Summer Flounder

Southern Flounder

Paralichthys lethostigma

RANGE: *Occurs statewide, except in extreme South Florida and Keys. The Southern is the common Flounder of virtually the entire Florida Atlantic Coast.*

HABITAT: *Most of the year, this fish is found in relatively shallow areas, preferring soft bottom near such cover as bars or rubble. Also holes in grass beds and edges of channels.*

DESCRIPTION: Brown or olive background, liberally marked with both dark blotches and white spots; however, the prominent eye-like spots (ocelli) of the Gulf Flounder are missing.

SIZE: This is the larger of Florida's two widely caught Flounders. It averages 2-4 pounds, but fish running 8-12 pounds are caught each year—mostly in the fall around major inlets from the Georgia line to Sebastian. World and Florida records 20 pounds, 9 ounces.

FOOD VALUE: One of the best.

GAME QUALITIES: Large fish get off some fair runs, but the outcome is seldom in doubt.

TACKLE AND BAITS: For most Flounder fishing, ordinary light spinning or baitcasting tackle is more than adequate. When targeting doormats around the inlets with live bait, the same types of gear, but with stouter rods and perhaps stronger lines should be used. Light saltwater boat tackle also does the job. Big Flounder are taken mostly with live fish as bait. Finger Mullet are favorites everywhere. Smaller fish—and big ones at times—will also hit live or dead shrimp and cut baits. While most fish-imitating lures will take Flounder, jigs are the most productive.

FISHING SYSTEMS: Still Fishing; Casting; Drifting.

Gulf Flounder
Paralichthys albigutta

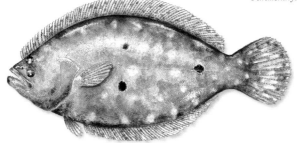

DESCRIPTION: Similar coloration to the Southern Flounder. Gulf Flounder's spots are three distinctive ocelli—eye-like spots.

SIZE: Averages 1-3 pounds, tops is 5 or 6. World record 6 pounds, 4 ounces.

FOOD VALUE: Among the best.

GAME QUALITIES: Moderate runs. Fun on light gear.

TACKLE AND BAITS: Light spinning, baitcasting.

FISHING SYSTEMS: Still Fishing; Casting; Drifting.

RANGE: *Statewide, but is the more common Flounder of the Gulf. Also, the few fair-sized Flounders that are caught in South Florida and the Keys are almost certainly this species.*

HABITAT: *Because giggers go after Gulf Flounder on shallow, sandy flats at night, many people think this is the top habitat. Anglers, however, are best advised to look for them near rocks or rubble.*

Summer Flounder "Fluke"
Paralichthys dentatus

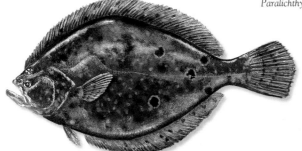

DESCRIPTION: Brownish or olive and heavily marked with spots of various colors.

SIZE: The largest of the three species, reaching 20 pounds, or even more. World record 22 pounds, 7 ounces.

FOOD VALUE: Excellent.

GAME QUALITIES: Fairly strong fighter on light line.

TACKLE AND BAITS: Same as for other flounders.

FISHING SYSTEMS: Inshore Still Fishing; Drift Fishing.

RANGE: *Extreme Northeast Florida. That's about the southernmost extent of its wanderings.*

HABITAT: *Same as Southern Flounder.*

Technically, of course, the fish in this chapter do belong to scientific families, but each is a sort of lone wolf, standing either as the only member of that particular family, or else the only member that is of importance in Florida. A couple of slight exceptions are the Tarpon and Ladyfish, which do belong to the same clan. Aside from the ocean-roaming Dolphin, most of these are at home in both deep and shallow water.

Three species of Barracuda are present in Florida and the islands, but two—the Sennet and the Guaguanche— are tiny. The Great Barracuda is the only one that stirs an angler's blood—sometimes with excitement and sometimes with anger. This is the fish of fable, the fierce marauder that, in early literature, was said to be more deadly than any shark. It's true that the spike-like teeth and swift striking ability of the Barracuda make it a fish to be treated with caution by fishermen, skin divers and swimmers alike, but it really isn't aggressive. While injuries have occurred from members of all three species named, most have been due to reckless or careless human behavior, and the rest to accidental contact.

As to the Dolphin, it would be hard to imagine a more nearly perfect fish—in the eyes of either a light-tackle angler or a seafood gourmet. This great fish is not only as aggressive and as strong as the biggest Jack, but as acrobatic as a Sailfish and as beautiful to look at as a tropical sunset. Moreover, you might argue that certain other species are as good in the culinary department, but it's doubtful there are any better. To top it all off, Dolphin are among the most numerous gamefish in the sea—reproducing fast and growing just as fast—and are the most convenient and easily caught of bluewater species.

Favorites Without Families

Great Barracuda

Bluefish

Bonefish

Cobia

Dolphin

Tarpon

Tripletail

Ladyfish

Great Barracuda

Sphyraena barracuda

OTHER NAMES:

Cuda

Sea Pike

Picuda

RANGE: *Florida coasts, the Bahamas and the Caribbean.*

HABITAT: *The Barracuda is at home almost anywhere in South Florida and the tropical islands—from shorelines and bays out to blue water. Although most fish in the shallows are small, it still is possible to connect with a 15- or 20-pounder—perhaps even a larger one—on the flats, or from shore. In Central and North Florida—both Atlantic and Gulf—the Great Barracuda is seldom seen inshore, but is common offshore on wrecks and artificial reefs.*

DESCRIPTION: Greenish or grayish above, with silvery sides marked by numerous dark blotches. Tail widely forked with pointed lobes. Two other members of the cuda family might be encountered. The fairly uncommon **Southern Sennet,** *Sphyraena picudilla,* grows to about 18 inches, but looks very similar to the bigger Cuda and is usually found in schools. The **Guaguanche,** *Sphyraena guachancho,* is much like the Sennet in size, shape and rarity. It can be distinguished by a yellow or gold mid-body stripe.

SIZE: The Great Barracuda ranges from foot-long juveniles on shallow flats to 50 pounds or more offshore. Usual maximum is around 30 pounds, with the average being 5-15 pounds. World record 85 pounds; Florida record 67 pounds.

FOOD VALUE: Excellent up to 5 pounds or so. Larger fish sometimes carry Ciguatera (see Introduction).

GAME QUALITIES: On appropriate tackle, the Great Barracuda is one of our most spectacular and able fighters, frequently mixing fast and fairly long runs with greyhounding jumps. In deeper water, such as over the reefs, it can also fight with strength and stamina.

TACKLE AND BAITS: For inshore fishing on the flats and along shorelines, spinning and baitcasting tackle are ideal, and fly tackle will also take plenty of Cuda. The best artificial bait for Barracuda is a tube lure, made from a foot or 18 inches of plastic tubing with wire through the middle and a hook on the end. Fly casters can make or buy similar lures of braided textile materials. Over reefs and wrecks, casting tackle is still a good choice, with light saltwater gear also capable of providing good sport. Live fish make the very best natural baits. The Barracuda also attacks rigged natural baits, such as Ballyhoo, with great pleasure.

FISHING SYSTEMS: Trolling; Casting; Still Fishing.

Bluefish

Pomatomus saltatrix

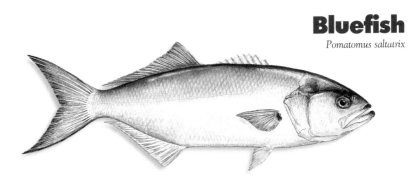

DESCRIPTION: Color is steel blue or dark green above, shading to silvery white below. Dark spot usually shows at base of pectoral fin. Large mouth with prominent teeth. Forked tail.

SIZE: Averages 1-3 pounds in most coastal waters of Florida, with catches to 6 or 7 pounds always possible, especially around major inlets, passes and jetties on both coasts. During runs of big fish, generally in the spring, Floridians have taken blues as heavy as 20 pounds or so. World record 31 pounds, 12 ounces; Florida record 22 pounds, 2 ounces.

FOOD VALUE: Small Bluefish make fine table fare if broiled or pan-fried soon after being landed—the same day if possible.

GAME QUALITIES: Outstanding fighter at all sizes. Strong runs and frequent jumps.

TACKLE AND BAITS: Light casting and spinning tackle is adequate in most instances, along with surf tackle for beach and pier fishing. Many big fish, during those aforementioned unpredictable runs, will put light trolling tackle to a good test. Heavy leaders are usually necessary to prevent clipoffs by the Blue's sharp teeth. Stout monofilament leaders usually suffice, but wire can be used too. Bluefish are ravenous as both predators and scavengers and will take virtually any popular bait—live and cut fish, cut squid, live shrimp. Fast-moving artificials work best, with the nod going to noisy surface plugs, jigs, spoons and swimming plugs, in about that order. Often, though, feeding Blues will slash at anything thrown their way.

FISHING SYSTEMS: Casting; Trolling; Still Fishing.

OTHER NAMES:
Blue
Chopper
Anchoa

RANGE: All Florida coasts.

HABITAT: Schools of small Bluefish roam outside beaches, bays and estuaries of both coasts—mostly summer in the upper half of Florida; fall and winter in the lower half. Many are caught each summer by anglers drifting shallow grass beds for Speckled Trout. Definite southward runs occur each year on both coasts, but they vary in size and extent. Runs of giant Blues—from 8 pounds to occasionally 20 or more, sometimes occur offshore and in the surf, usually in March and April on the Atlantic Coast and in late summer or fall in the Panhandle, but these are unpredictable.

Bonefish

Albula vulpes

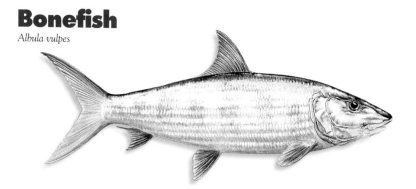

OTHER NAMES:

Silver Ghost
White Fox
Macabi

RANGE: The bonefish is a tropical species and is seriously fished only in the south end of Biscayne Bay, Greater Miami and the Florida Keys—and also, of course, throughout the Bahamas and Caribbean. Stragglers are sometimes caught north of the preferred habitat, usually from the surf, although a few are taken from the Indian River. The Longfin variety is rare in Florida.

HABITAT: Bonefish do much of their foraging on shallow mud or grass flats, where they can be sighted and cast to. They also frequently gather in large schools over fairly deep, soft bottom, where their feeding stirs up patches of silt or "mud."

DESCRIPTION: Thick-bodied but streamlined. Dark back, usually greenish, and silver sides; pointed snout with underslung mouth; forked tail. A smaller and much lesser-known variety, the **Longfin Bonefish, *Albula nemoptera,*** looks almost identical, except for streamer-like extensions of its dorsal and anal fins.

SIZE: Common from 2 to 10 pounds; sometimes to 15 pounds, and possibly to 18 or 20. World record 19 pounds; Florida record 15 pounds, 12 ounces.

FOOD VALUE: Although popular in the Bahamas and tropics, Bonefish are seldom eaten in Florida. They are indeed very bony; and too highly prized as gamefish to kill for, at best, a mediocre dinner.

GAME QUALITIES: Legendary for long-distance runs in shallow water. Strong, jack-like fighter in deep water.

TACKLE AND BAITS: For sight-fishing in the classic style, the most productive tackle is a spinning outfit with a light rod of 7 feet or longer and 8-pound-test line. Bonefish are also among the top favorites of fly fishermen, whose standard gear is an 8-weight outfit. Lighter fly rods get some spot use, if wind conditions allow, and 9-weight outfits are not too heavy for good sport. Live shrimp is the bait of choice among spin fishermen, but cut shrimp, conch (in the Bahamas and Caribbean) and crab all work well. Best lures are "skimmer" jigs, 1/8 or 1/4 ounce, with horizontally flattened heads that help keep the hook upright. Most fly rodders lean toward very small flies with monofilament weedguards on No. 2 or even No. 4 hooks, but standard streamers on No. 1 or 1/0 hooks work. In a less-than-classic approach, Bonefish can be caught by bottom fishing on deep flats and in channels near the flats.

FISHING SYSTEMS: Casting; Still Fishing.

Cobia

Rachycentron canadum

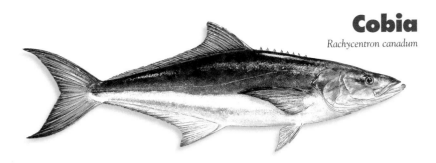

DESCRIPTION: In the water, Cobia look very much like sharks. The usual color is brown or dark gray above, whitish on the underside, with a dark stripe running from gills to base of tail. The striped appearance is more vivid in juveniles. Several rather sharp finlets on the dorsal surface extend from behind the head to the dorsal fin.

SIZE: Common from 20 to 50 pounds; sometimes up to 80 pounds, and possibly to 100 or more. World record 135 pounds, 9 ounces; Florida record 130 pounds, 1 ounces.

FOOD VALUE: Excellent, smoked or fresh.

GAME QUALITIES: A strong but unpredictable fighter. Usually clicks off fairly long, fast runs, and can fight deep with great stamina; however, many individuals put on lackluster fights if not pressured too hard—saving their best efforts for after they are boated!

TACKLE AND BAITS: Surf tackle is the best bet for pier fishing—and for boat fishing when long casts with heavy lures are called for. Since Cobia are notorious for wrapping lines around buoys and wreck structure, most anglers use 30-pound-test line or heavier. Once clear of obstructions, however, even large Cobia can be successfully fought with spinning, baitcasting and fly tackle—although a minimum of 10-pound line or tippet is advisable. When gaffed "green" (not tired), Cobia can—and often do—smash up the inside of a boat. Jigs and large streamer flies are the most-used artificials. Spoons and swimming plugs often work well; you might wake them up with a surface plug, popper or tube lure. Live baitfish, such as Pinfish, Mullet, Cigar Minnows, Grunts and Jacks work best, but live shrimp, crabs, dead fish or squid are good too.

FISHING SYSTEMS: Still Fishing; Casting; Trolling; Drifting.

OTHER NAMES:
Ling
Crab Eater
Lemonfish
Bacalao

RANGE: All Florida coasts; widespread throughout the Bahamas and Caribbean, although seldom plentiful.

HABITAT: All the way from shallow inshore waters to the deep sea. Most Florida Cobia winter in the southern reaches of the state or offshore, migrating northward in the Spring to cover both coasts. Dramatic runs occur along Panhandle beaches in April. Cobia love to hang around navigation markers, wrecks and artificial reefs, where they swim both at the surface and down deep. They also escort wandering Mantas and other large rays, and many are caught around those hosts. Juveniles are frequently caught incidentally by trout fishermen over many Gulf Coast grass flats—and some big ones too.

Dolphin

Coryphaena hippurus

OTHER NAMES:

Dorado

Mahi Mahi

RANGE: *All offshore waters of Florida, the Bahamas and the Caribbean.*

HABITAT: *Dolphin roam the open sea in a continuous hunt for food. Anglers seek them along rafted weedlines and around any sort of large floating object. The location of schools may also be given away by feeding birds, particularly frigate birds.*

DESCRIPTION: A blaze of blue and yellow or deep green and yellow when in the water, and sometimes shows dark vertical stripes as well when excited. Small dark spots on sides. Dorsal fin extends nearly from head to tail. Head is very blunt in males (bulls); rounded in females (cows). The **Pompano Dolphin,** *Coryphaena equisetis,* is often mistaken as a female or juvenile male Dolphin. It is found in most of the same waters, grows to about 5 pounds and can be distinguished by the rounded shape of the underbelly.

SIZE: Schooling fish run in similar sizes, from around a pound to nearly 20 pounds at times; larger fish are loners, or else pairs—bull and cow. Big bulls often reach 50 pounds in weight and can exceed 80 pounds on rare occasion. Large cows generally top out at 40 pounds or so. World record 88 pounds; Florida record 77 pounds, 12 ounces.

FOOD VALUE: None better.

GAME QUALITIES: Top of the heap in any weight class—speedy. Strong and acrobatic.

TACKLE AND BAITS: With the Dolphin, anything goes. Private-boat anglers seek to find a school by trolling or by running and searching for visual signs. Once a school is located, it can usually be kept around the boat by restrained chumming with cut bait and/or by keeping at least one hooked fish in the water at all times. A hot school will eagerly accept jigs and all sorts of casting baits, including flies and popping bugs. If strikes slow down, cut bait often does the trick. Big or wise fish may insist on live baits. Countless Dolphin are also caught, both by design and incidentally, on the entire gamut of rigged trolling baits and artificial trolling lures.

FISHING SYSTEMS: Trolling; Drifting; Casting.

Tarpon

Megalops atlanticus

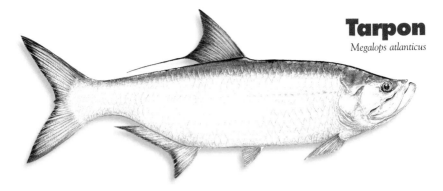

DESCRIPTION: Green or steel blue above, silver on sides and belly. Deep, thick body; forked tail. Long trailer at end of dorsal fin.

SIZE: From 12 inches or less to about 75 pounds, on average, although big fish of 100 to 150 pounds are numerous in many areas. World record 286 pounds, 9 ounces; Florida record 243 pounds.

FOOD VALUE: None.

GAME QUALITIES: Famous for the spectacle and frequency of its jumps. Giant Tarpon don't quite match the acrobatics of the smaller ones, but they leap frequently enough in shallow water, and with even more fury.

TACKLE AND BAITS: Anglers seeking big fish in passes, channels, deep bays and surf areas like stout tackle with lines testing at least 30 pounds. All sizes of spinning, baitcasting and fly tackle get lots of play for smaller fish. The same types of gear, although of heavier proportions, are also used for big fish on shallow flats. Use at least 15-pound line on spinning and casting gear, and at least a 10-weight fly outfit with minimum 16-pound tippet. Heavy monofilament leaders or tippets are required because of the Tarpon's very rough mouth. Drift-fishermen in the passes and inlets prefer live baits—mainly small crabs and small fish. All Tarpon will take dead baits, such as a Mullet head or half Mullet, fished patiently on bottom. For trolling or surfcasting with heavier gear, large jigs, spoons and lipped plugs get the call. Generally, casters enjoy the most success with swimming plugs, jerk plugs and surface plugs. Fly fishermen rely heavily on scissor-action feather streamers and bulky bucktail streamers.

FISHING SYSTEMS: Casting; Drifting; Still Fishing; Trolling.

OTHER NAMES:
Silver King
Sabalo

RANGE: *All Florida coasts plus the Greater Antilles and some other Caribbean islands, including the Virgin and Cayman Islands. Scattered in the Bahamas, where it is most plentiful around Andros but also present elsewhere, including Bimini, the Berry Islands, and the Exumas.*

HABITAT: *Fishable throughout Florida in warm months, including the Panhandle, but adults are largely confined to South Florida in the winter. Major fishing efforts for big Tarpon are directed at live-baiting in large passes, inlets, channels and river mouths throughout the state, and at sight-fishing with fly and casting tackle on shallow flats in the Keys and on the lower Gulf Coast from Homosassa southward. Large and medium Tarpon also are found off the beaches and in the surf of both coasts at times, and many are hooked from bridges and piers, especially at night. Medium-size fish are common in a variety of settings in South and Central Florida, including freshwater rivers and landlocked canals. Tiny juveniles inhabit landlocked canals and ditches.*

Tripletail

Lobotes surinamensis

OTHER NAMES:

Drift Fish
Leaf Fish

RANGE: Both coastal and pelagic in Florida; mostly pelagic in the Bahamas and Caribbean.

HABITAT: The Tripletail is a true world traveler, drifting with ocean currents and often spotted by dolphin fishermen in weedlines or alongside floating debris. Many are found closer to shore in most coastal areas of Florida during warm months, and also in larger bays—usually hanging around markers or trap floats.

DESCRIPTION: Deep, somewhat rounded shape gives it the appearance of an oversize panfish. Color varies but is usually brownish and mottled. Head is concave above the mouth. Name derives from similarity and near juxtaposition of the dorsal, caudal and anal fins, resembling three tails.

SIZE: Most run 2-12 pounds; but rare catches reach 30 or more. World record 42 pounds, 5 ounces; Florida record 40 pounds, 13 ounces.

FOOD VALUE: One of the best.

GAME QUALITIES: Despite its clumsy looks, the Tripletail is a good gamefish in all respects. It willingly strikes artificial lures and its fight is characterized by short, frantic runs and startling jumps. Big ones in deep water are also good at bulldogging. Like Cobia—with which they frequently share the shade of a navigation structure—Tripletail are adept at fouling lines.

TACKLE AND BAITS: Casting tackle—fly, plug or spinning—provides the best and most spectacular sport with Tripletails, but saltwater outfits with lines up to 30-pound test are not out of place for big fish in tight places. Streamer flies, plastic and bucktail jigs and mirror plugs are among the pet lures. Best natural baits are live shrimp and small live fish. Strip baits and dead shrimp are also taken.

FISHING SYSTEMS: Still Fishing; Drifting; Casting.

Ladyfish

Elops saurus

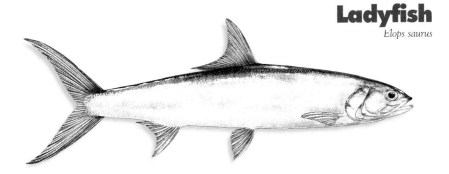

DESCRIPTION: A slender, silvery fish with deeply forked tail and large, scoop-shaped lower jaw. Said to be mistaken at times for the Bonefish, but the error is difficult to conceive of, given the big mouth and jumping ability of the Ladyfish.

SIZE: Usually 1-2 pounds; 3-4-pound Ladyfish are whoppers. Reported to reach even more, but very rarely. World record 8 pounds; Florida record 6 pounds.

FOOD VALUE: Edible but not very appetizing; many bones and flesh is mushy.

GAME QUALITIES: One of the wildest acrobats, always getting off spectacular and frequent jumps. Larger ones are strong pullers and can uncork surprisingly long runs.

TACKLE AND BAITS: Scrappy on any light casting tackle, including fly. Great sport with ultralight gear. Most are caught on cut strips, small live fish or live shrimp by anglers fishing for something else, particularly for Trout on the flats, but Ladyfish are ready strikers on most artificial lures of appropriate size. Jigs and small topwater plugs rate high, as do popping bugs and small white streamer flies.

FISHING SYSTEMS: Casting; Drifting; Still Fishing.

OTHER NAMES:
Ten-Pounder
Skipjack
Chiro

RANGE: All Florida coasts, the Bahamas and Caribbean.

HABITAT: Ladyfish occur the full length of both coasts, ranging from the open sea off beaches and shorelines, to inlets and bays, and far up coastal streams. They seem to have no preferred surroundings, but follow wherever good feeding conditions take them—whether over shallow flats or in deep holes and channels. They love to feed at night and are common around lighted areas of piers and docks. They often gather in large schools.

The Jack family is a huge one that ranks among the most important groups of sporting fish. In Florida, it is rivaled in number, distribution, diversity and angler interest only by the Mackerel-Tuna family. That statement might surprise fishermen who, whenever the word "Jack" is mentioned, tend to think only of the Crevalle, but the group includes some of the most famous names among sport fish, as well as some of the most infamous. Among the upper crust are those family members that wear labels other than Jack—prestigious titles like Pompano, Permit, Amberjack and African Pompano. At the other end of the scale are representatives like the Blue Runner and Lookdown— smaller fish that serve the angling world well, whether as light-tackle battlers or as bait for larger species. Jacks typically are smooth-skinned, or have scales so tiny that the skin appears smooth. Most of them have narrow caudal peduncles that are covered with hard, and often fairly sharp, scaly ridges called scutes. The caudal peduncle is soft, however, in the Pompanos and Amberjacks.

The Jacks

Crevalle Jack

Blue Runner

Bar Jack

Yellow Jack

Horse-Eye Jack

Rainbow Runner

Leatherjack

Pilotfish

Greater Amberjack

Lesser Amberjack

Almaco Jack

Banded Rudderfish

Florida Pompano

Permit

Palometa

African Pompano

Lookdown

Crevalle Jack

Caranx hippos

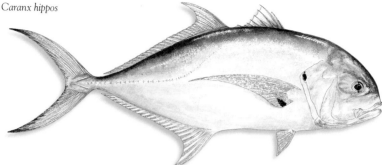

OTHER NAMES:
Jack Crevalle
Crevally

RANGE: *All Florida and the Greater Antilles; rare in the Bahamas and smaller Caribbean Islands.*

HABITAT: *The Crevalle may show up at any time in virtually all Florida waters, from the deep reefs to well up coastal rivers. Usually runs in schools—and the smaller the individual fish, the larger the school. The biggest Jacks often cruise in pairs and are usually found in or near major inlets and around offshore wrecks and reefs of both coasts, but may come into deep bays and canals where they chase Mullet and often herd the prey against seawalls. The Palm Beaches and Key West are particularly well-known areas for trophy Crevalles.*

DESCRIPTION: Deep, compressed body. Blunt head with black spot on rear edge of gill cover. Hard scutes forward of sickle-shaped tail. Color usually yellowish with white undersides.

SIZE: Common at 1 pound or less to about 5 or 6 pounds. Plentiful up to 12 pounds in most areas. Sometimes tops 20 pounds and can reach 50 pounds or even more. World record 58 pounds, 6 ounces.

FOOD VALUE: Poor by most tastes. Most of the meat is dark red and of strong flavor.

GAME QUALITIES: Few fish can out-pull a Crevalle of equal size. The fight is unspectacular but dogged, the usual pattern being a long first run. Jacks use their flat sides to good advantage when waging a tug-o-war.

TACKLE AND BAITS: Most Jacks are fairly small and are caught on the full range of light tackle by anglers seeking other game. If you target larger Jacks, say 10 pounds or more, sturdy spinning, baitcasting and fly tackle should be used, with lines no less than 8-pound test. Small Jacks, such as those frequently encountered on shallow flats, will gulp down almost any sort of natural bait, live or dead, as well as all the popular casting and flyrod lures. Big Crevalles, however, generally like their meals moving very fast. To assure hookups, you have to use fresh and frisky live fish, or retrieve your artificial lures rapidly, noisily, or both. Topwater plugs are good, as are fast-whipped jigs. Fly rodders often have to work very hard, stripping their streamers or poppers as fast as their elbows will move.

FISHING SYSTEMS: Casting; Trolling; Drifting; Still Fishing.

Blue Runner

Caranx crysos

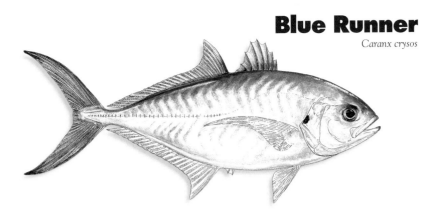

DESCRIPTION: Similar in shape to the Crevalle, but with a more gently rounded head. Color ranges from steel blue to light green with white underparts. Hard scutes forward of tail.

SIZE: Schooling Blue Runners are about the same size, averaging under a pound and often under a half-pound. Fish weighing 1-2 pounds aren't unusual, and individuals up to 4 pounds or so are sometimes taken offshore. World record 11 pounds, 2 ounces; Florida record 8 pounds, 5 ounces.

FOOD VALUE: Pretty good, but seldom eaten.

GAME QUALITIES: Blue Runners fight so well for their size that guides often have trouble tearing their customers away, after stopping to catch some Runners on spinning tackle for use as offshore bait.

TACKLE AND BAITS: Light spinning and fly tackle with live shrimp, cut pieces of fish or small artificial jigs and flies.

FISHING SYSTEMS: Trolling; Drifting; Casting; Still Fishing.

OTHER NAMES:
Hardtail Jack
Runner
Blue Jack

RANGE: All Florida, the Bahamas and the Caribbean.

HABITAT: Not choosy; inshore to deep sea.

Bar Jack

Caranx ruber

RANGE: Common in the Bahamas and Caribbean; also found in South Florida.

HABITAT: Likes sandy beach areas, clear, grassy flats and coral reefs.

DESCRIPTION: Streamlined shape. Hard scutes forward of tail. Bright blue and black topside with silvery sides and a thin deep-purple stripe extending from behind the head into the lower lobe of the tail.

SIZE: Averages a pound or so. Reaches at least 5 pounds on occasion. World and Florida records 7 pounds, 12 ounces.

FOOD VALUE: Excellent; less red meat than most Jacks.

GAME QUALITIES: Though usually small, fights as if twice or more its size.

TACKLE AND BAITS: Most sport will be obtained with light spinning tackle. Also a good fly fish, again with lighter outfits. Takes live shrimp, live minnows, Bonefish jigs and flies and other small lures.

FISHING SYSTEMS: Casting; Trolling; Drifting; Still Fishing.

Yellow Jack

Caranx bartholomaei

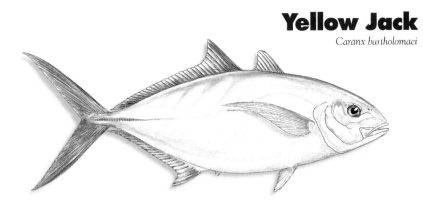

DESCRIPTION: More streamlined in appearance than the Crevalle, and more colorful. Hard scutes forward of tail. Color is bluish above, yellowish on sides. Small Yellow Jacks have fins and tails of bright yellow, giving them the appearance of yellowtail snapper when seen from above the surface.

SIZE: Averages 1-6 pounds; not uncommon at 12-15 pounds; grows to about 20 pounds. World record 19 pounds, 7 ounces.

FOOD VALUE: Excellent. Red meat along the center-line is easily trimmed away, leaving white, flavorful fillets.

GAME QUALITIES: Like other Jacks, a rugged and persevering fighter.

TACKLE AND BAITS: Spinning, baitcasting and light saltwater outfits will give good sport. Small live fish, particularly Ballyhoo and Pilchards are the best natural baits. Biggest Bar Jack have been caught on top-water plugs over channels and shallow reefs, and on deep jigs in up to about 120 feet of water. On the flats, the bigger Bar Jack are moody but smaller ones eagerly hit live shrimp, Bonefish jigs and other small lures.

FISHING SYSTEMS: Casting; Trolling; Drifting; Still Fishing.

OTHER NAMES:
Bar Jack
Cibi Amarillo

RANGE: Common in southern Florida, the Bahamas and the Caribbean.

HABITAT: Inshore flats and channels; coral reefs.

Horse-eye Jack

Caranx latus

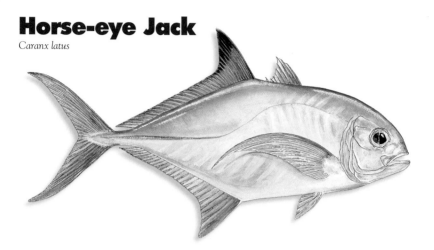

Bigeye Jack
Ojo Gordo

RANGE: All Florida, especially South Florida—but more common in the Bahamas and Caribbean.

HABITAT: More of an open-water species than the Crevalle, it is found over the reefs and near the beaches; also in channels and harbors.

DESCRIPTION: Similar in body shape to the Crevalle, but the head is not quite so blunt. The color is also different, being usually silvery on the sides and below; dark gray or blackish above. The fins are blackish as opposed to the yellow tinge of the Crevalle. Hard scutes forward of tail. As the name indicates, the eyes are very large.

SIZE: Commonly caught in similar sizes to the Crevalle, but does not grow so large, topping out at 20 pounds or so. World and Florida records 25 pounds, 12 ounces.

FOOD VALUE: Poor by most tastes, and has been implicated in Ciguatera poisoning (see Introduction).

GAME QUALITIES: Like the Crevalle, a tough brawler.

TACKLE AND BAITS: See Jack Crevalle.

FISHING SYSTEMS: Casting; Trolling; Drifting.

Rainbow Runner

Elagatis bipinnulata

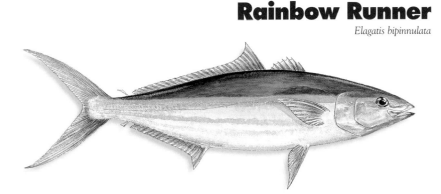

DESCRIPTION: Un-jack-like streamlined shape with slender, pointed head. No hard scutes forward of tail. Brilliantly colored, with blue and yellow full-length stripes on a blue background.

SIZE: Varies from a couple of pounds to 15 or 20 pounds, with individuals of roughly the same size forming large schools. World record 37 pounds, 9 ounces; Florida record 23 pounds.

FOOD VALUE: Excellent.

GAME QUALITIES: A spirited fighter on light tackle. Makes faster runs than other Jacks, and sometimes jumps, too.

TACKLE AND BAITS: Spinning, baitcasting and light ocean rigs. Small live fish and small rigged baits, such as Ballyhoo and strips. Difficult to take by casting, but can be coaxed.

FISHING SYSTEMS: Trolling; Casting.

OTHER NAMES:
Spanish Jack
Rainbow Jack

RANGE: Not a staple species off Florida, but often encountered by offshore anglers of both coasts, particularly Dolphin fishermen. More common in Bahamas waters, particularly around the Cay Sal Bank; also widespread through the Caribbean.

HABITAT: Deep ocean waters.

Leatherjack

Oligoplites saurus

OTHER NAMES:
Leatherjacket
Skipjack
Zapetero

RANGE: *All Florida and the Greater Antilles.*

HABITAT: *Open water of Gulf and Atlantic; also in bays and up coastal rivers. A schooling species, it's often found in company with schools of Spanish Mackerel or Jacks, feeding on the same small fry as the larger fish.*

DESCRIPTION: Slender, compressed shape with pointed head and large jaws for its size. Leathery skin is green above and silvery on the sides. Sharp spines on dorsal and anal fins can administer very painful puncture wounds.

SIZE: A few inches, rarely as much as a foot.

FOOD VALUE: None.

GAME QUALITIES: Poor.

TACKLE AND BAITS: The Leatherjack will take many different small baits and lures offered for Mackerel and other desirable species.

FISHING SYSTEMS: Not fished for deliberately.

Pilotfish

Naucrates ductor

RANGE: *All Florida, the Bahamas and Caribbean.*

HABITAT: *Offshore waters. Name comes from accompanying sharks and other large animals—seemingly as pilots.*

DESCRIPTION: Slender shape with tapering head. Body marked by wide, dark bands. Fins also banded.

SIZE: Usually a foot or so; grows to 2 feet.

FOOD VALUE: Good, if fish is large enough.

GAME QUALITIES: Good on light tackle; gives the fight of a typical small Jack.

TACKLE AND BAITS: Readily takes small jigs and streamer flies. Only very light outfits provide much sport.

FISHING SYSTEMS: Offshore drifting.

Greater Amberjack

Seriola dumerili

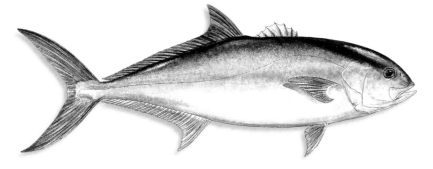

DESCRIPTION: Overall brownish or goldish. Heavy body. No scutes forward of tail fin. Dark oblique line through the eye that ends at the dorsal fin.

SIZE: Schools of young fish are common at 5-20 pounds. Average size over deep wrecks and reefs is 30-60 pounds, but 100-pounders are not too rare and the potential maximum exceeds 150 pounds. World record 155 pounds, 10 ounces; Florida record 142 pounds.

FOOD VALUE: Excellent, smoked or fresh.

GAME QUALITIES: A strong, punishing fighter that powers deep and defies lifting. Fairly long runs can also occur early in the fight. A great deal of stamina matches their strength. Novices may fight Amberjack of average size for an hour or longer.

TACKLE AND BAITS: Amberjack are most often caught aboard charterboats and partyboats on heavy rods and reels with lines testing 50 pounds or more—and are no patsies, even then. Experienced light-tackle anglers can successfully battle them with spinning and baitcasting rigs, and even fly rods. Around wrecks, they frequently follow hooked fish to boatside, and also may rise to the top voluntarily. Then they can be cast to with surface plugs, spoons, jigs, or big flyrod streamers and poppers. Live chum will also draw Amberjack from the depths. Best bait with heavy tackle is any sort of live fish, the friskier the better.

FISHING SYSTEMS: Drifting; Trolling; Casting.

OTHER NAMES:
Amberfish
AJ
Coronado
Cavilia

RANGE: All Florida, the Bahamas and Caribbean.

HABITAT: Adults are common at various depths, ranging from reefs several hundred feet deep to fairly shallow wrecks and reefs. Big ones also come close to shore at times, particularly in the Keys and the Islands. Artificial reefs and wrecks all along the Gulf Coast often harbor huge schools of smaller Amberjack, and many Gulf wrecks are home to big ones as well.

Lesser Amberjack

Seriola fasciata

RANGE: *All Florida, the Bahamas and Caribbean.*

HABITAT: *The Lesser Amberjack is not common. Most that have been definitely identified came from well offshore, usually around weedlines and flotsam. May occur inshore as well, although the huge majority of very small Amberjack caught around Gulf wrecks in Florida are simply juveniles of the Great Amberjack, Seriola dumerili.*

DESCRIPTION: Almost a dead ringer for the Greater Amberjack, except for size, but only the very smallest of the big species would be confused. The most obvious difference is that the band through the eye of the Lesser Amberjack stops noticeably forward of the dorsal fin.

SIZE: Seldom, perhaps never, exceeds 12 inches.

FOOD VALUE: Minimal.

GAME QUALITIES: At least as good as other Jacks.

TACKLE AND BAITS: Ultralight spinning and fly tackle. Small jigs, plugs and flies.

FISHING SYSTEMS: Drifting; Still Fishing.

Almaco Jack

Seriola rivoliana

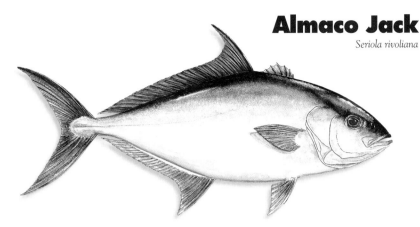

DESCRIPTION: Similar at a glance to the Great Amberjack, due to coloring and the presence of the band through the eye, but there are glaring differences upon closer inspection. The body of the Almaco is deep and more compressed; also, the dorsal and anal fins are longer and sickle-shaped.

SIZE: Common to 15 pounds; sometimes exceeds 30 pounds. World record 78 pounds.

FOOD VALUE: Excellent. Best prepared by skinning, filleting and trimming away the dark portions.

GAME QUALITIES: As tough as the Great Amberjack.

TACKLE AND BAITS: Spinning, baitcasting and light ocean tackle with lines up to 20-pound test are ideal; however, since most Almacos are caught in Amberjack habitat, heavier gear often is used. Small live baits are seldom refused. Jigs work too, provided they are given fast action by the fisherman.

FISHING SYSTEMS: Drifting; Still Fishing.

OTHER NAMES:
Almaco

RANGE: All Florida, the Bahamas and Caribbean.

HABITAT: Largely the same as the Great Amberjack—reefs and wrecks. Curiously, a particular wreck often seems to hold one species or the other, but both are present in many spots.

Banded Rudderfish

Seriola zonata

OTHER NAMES:

Slender Amberjack

RANGE: All Florida, the Bahamas and Caribbean.

HABITAT: Unlike the pelagic Pilotfish, the Banded Rudderfish is more coastal and prefers reef habitat. May also be found around navigation aids and in deep channels.

DESCRIPTION: Easily confused with the Pilotfish because both have dark vertical bands, but the Banded Rudderfish is a small type of Amberjack—as evidenced by the dark line through the eye, which the Pilotfish does not have.

SIZE: Usually a foot or less; grows to perhaps 2 feet.

FOOD VALUE: Excellent, particularly if large enough to render small fillets.

GAME QUALITIES: Typical of its family, the Banded Rudderfish is aggressive and will strike with abandon. Its battle is much like that of a Blue Runner—tough for its size.

TACKLE AND BAITS: Seldom targeted, but if action is slow and a school presents itself, the angler can try very light spinning, baitcasting or fly outfits, with small jigs, spoons or streamer flies. Rudderfish will also take any live baitfish of suitable size, as well as live shrimp and small strips of squid or cut fish.

FISHING SYSTEMS: Drifting; Still Fishing.

Florida Pompano

Trachinotus carolinus

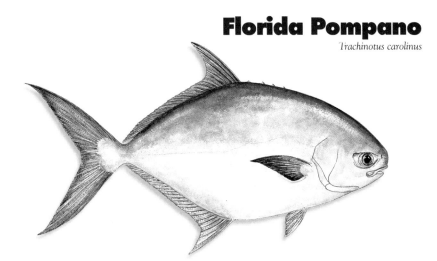

DESCRIPTION: Silvery overall with yellow on underside. Dorsal fin dark; other fins yellow. Head gently rounded. No scutes forward of tail. Pompano are often confused with small Permit of similar size, but Permit usually show a black blotch under the pectoral fin, and their bodies are deeper.

SIZE: Averages 1 pound; fairly common at 2 pounds and can grow to 8 pounds. World and Florida records 8 pounds, 4 ounces.

FOOD VALUE: Reputed to be the best.

GAME QUALITIES: Tops. Will outrace and outpull a Jack Crevalle of equivalent size.

TACKLE AND BAITS: If fishing the surf or piers, use the lightest surf spinning tackle that will get your bait where you want it. In other situations, spinning or light baitcasting tackle with 6-8-pound-test line gives maximum sport. By far the best natural bait is a live sand flea (sand crab), but Pompano also will bite live shrimp or fiddler crabs and—with varying dependability—dead sand fleas, dead shrimp, clams and cut squid. Pompano are ready strikers of artificial jigs, the Florida favorite being quarter-ounce or half-ounce models with short nylon skirts. Fly fishermen catch Pompano with Bonefish-type flies that sink well—those with epoxy heads or lead eyes.

FISHING SYSTEMS: Still Fishing; Casting; Drifting.

OTHER NAMES:
Pompano
Carolina Pompano

RANGE: All Florida coasts.

HABITAT: Florida anglers on both coasts catch most of their Pompano from the surf, or from ocean piers; however, many are caught outside the beaches and also from bays, mostly in or near channels that run through flats.

Permit

Trachinotus falcatus

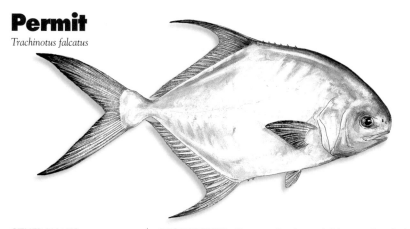

OTHER NAMES:

Round Pompano
Great Pompano

RANGE: *All Florida, the Bahamas and Caribbean.*

HABITAT: *Permit are found in the surf, inlets and passes of both coasts, but are more numerous in the southern half of the state. In warm weather, they roam South Atlantic reefs and many Gulf wrecks. "Classic" Permit stalking on the flats is largely confined to Dade County and the Florida Keys, as well as the Bahamas and Caribbean.*

DESCRIPTION: Deeper body and blunter head than the Pompano. Large, sickle-shaped tail. Scutes absent. Silver overall; sometimes has a black blotch on side under the pectoral fin. Like Pompano, small Permit may also show some yellow on the underside.

SIZE: Can run as high as 40 or 50 pounds, with 20-30-pounders fairly common. World record 60 pounds; Florida record 56 pounds, 2 ounces.

FOOD VALUE: When small enough to be confused with Pompano, the confusion extends to the table. Both are excellent.

GAME QUALITIES: Rates as one of the very best game-fish—a long runner on the flats and a strong, stubborn deep fighter offshore. Also one of the most challenging to fool, especially with artificial lures.

TACKLE AND BAITS: Although offshore Permit are large enough to provide sport with light and medium saltwater tackle, the epitome of Permit fishing is to stalk them by sight on shallow flats, and cast directly to them. Light spinning, baitcasting and fly tackle can be used in the shallows—provided the angler has a good supply of line and a means (a guide with a push-pole, preferably) of chasing the fish. Best natural bait is any sort of small live crab. Dead pieces of crab and lobster also work well. Live shrimp are often accept-ed, especially if skittered across the surface, and then allowed to sink. If using small skimmer (Bonefish-style) jigs, try to get the Permit to follow the lure, then stop it dead and let it sink into the grass or mud. Best flies are those with weighted or epoxy heads that will sink in the manner of a leadhead jig.

FISHING SYSTEMS: Casting; Still Fishing.

Palometa

Trachinotus goodei

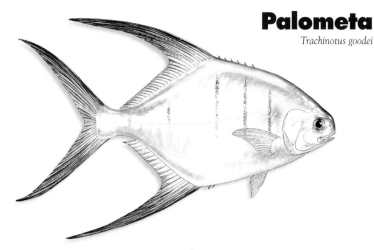

DESCRIPTION: Elongated rays of the dorsal and anal fin, along with vertical dark bars that are visible both in and out of the water make this Pompano easy to name.

SIZE: From less than a pound to possibly 2 pounds. World record 1 pound, 12 ounces.

FOOD VALUE: Like all the Pompanos, excellent. Can be dressed and either baked or sautéed in a pan.

GAME QUALITIES: The size may be small but the fight is spirited on light tackle, and runs can be zippy. This fish is also wary and often hard to fool.

TACKLE AND BAITS: The lightest spinning and fly tackle with jigs and flies tied on No. 1 or smaller hooks. Small crabs, sand fleas and shrimp are top baits.

FISHING SYSTEMS: Still Fishing; Casting.

OTHER NAMES:

Longfin Pompano
Pompanito
Gafftopsail Pompano

RANGE: The Bahamas, Caribbean and South Florida.

HABITAT: Likes clear water with sandy bottom. Quite common along sheltered beaches and sandbars of many islands. Now becoming rather scarce in Florida.

African Pompano
Alectis ciliaris

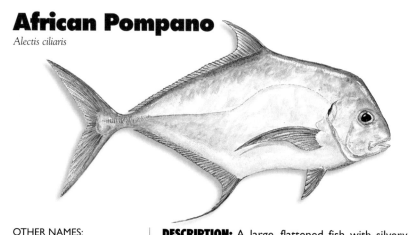

Threadfish
Cuban Jack
Flechudo

RANGE: *Most African Pompano are encountered on the lower half of the Atlantic Coast and in the Keys. They also are found throughout the Bahamas and Caribbean.*

HABITAT: *The young prefer shallow reefs. Adults may be found over shallow reefs as well, but tend to work deeper as they grow. Best fishing grounds are usually around deep wrecks.*

DESCRIPTION: A large, flattened fish with silvery or pearlescent sides and a distinctive blunt, steeply sloped head. Forward rays of the dorsal and anal fins are very long and threadlike in young fish, and these "streamers" sometimes hang on until adulthood, although they usually are lost as the fish grows.

SIZE: The smallest specimens have the longest fins, and young "Threadfish" of a couple pounds and less were once thought to be a different species. Adults are common at 15-30 pounds and grow to at least 50 pounds. World and Florida records 50 pounds, 8 ounces.

FOOD VALUE: Excellent.

GAME QUALITIES: One of the toughest light-tackle customers around, the African fights much like other big Jacks, but uses its flat side to even greater advantage, and exhibits a peculiar, circling tactic that puts the angler to a thorough test.

TACKLE AND BAITS: As one of the pets of the light-tackle fraternity, most African Pompano are caught by jigging deep in the vicinity of wrecks or offshore dropoffs with spinning and baitcasting tackle; or by fishing deep with light ocean tackle and live bait. They generally hang too deep to interest fly fishermen, although a few have been caught by blind-fishing over wrecks with sinking lines, or by chumming them to the surface with live chum. A variety of heavy jigs and large streamers will work, especially if trimmed with silvery Mylar. Pinfish, Pilchards and similar small fish are the live baits of choice. Africans are occasionally caught by trolling over the reefs with feathers or rigged baits.

FISHING SYSTEMS: Drifting; Trolling; Still Fishing.

Lookdown

Selene vomer

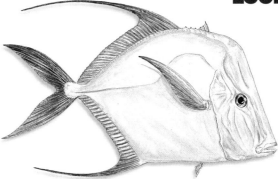

DESCRIPTION: Both the Lookdown and the **Atlantic Moonfish,** *Selene setapinnis,* are flat, silvery fish of similar size, appearance and habits. Moreover, they are often found in company with each other, which adds to the angler's confusion. The Lookdown has a sloping, concave head and long streamers running off the dorsal and anal fins. These streamers, however, are not nearly so long and flowing as those of the juvenile African Pompano. The head of the Moonfish is less blunted than that of the Lookdown, and all its fins are short.

SIZE: Both run from hand size to more than 1 pound. World record 4 pounds, 12 ounces.

FOOD VALUE: Excellent panfish.

GAME QUALITIES: Both are aggressive strikers and spirited fighters for their size.

TACKLE AND BAITS: When a good spot has been identified, ultralight or very light spinning and fly tackle provides the most sport. Both fish are good strikers on small jigs and tiny plugs. They also take live minnows and shrimp, but don't much care for dead baits.

FISHING SYSTEMS: Casting; Still Fishing.

OTHER NAMES:

Jorobado
Horse-head

RANGE: All Florida, the Bahamas and Caribbean.

HABITAT: Lookdown and Moonfish may be found nearly anywhere in shallow coastal waters, but are most common around bridge and dock pilings, navigation markers, and in channels and canals, where they frequently gather under shoreside lights at night.

Few families of fish are as widely appreciated throughout Florida and the islands as the Snappers. The reason is a happy (for the successful angler) combination of gameness and table appeal, plus their willingness to take a variety of baits. Despite their appetites, however, most Snappers can be among the wariest of biters when visibility is good enough to permit a close look at terminal tackle.

All the Snappers are hard fighters that generally wage a strong, head-shaking tug-of-war against the angler, and those caught in shallow water are also capable of making long and surprisingly fast runs. Numerous members of the family occur from the inshore shallows to as far out in the ocean depths as man will ever fish.

With only a couple of exceptions, noted in the descriptions, the Snappers can be identified as family members by their prominent canine teeth. Some, the Gray or Mangrove Snapper in particular, routinely snap at the angler's hands with apparent viciousness—a habit that gave rise to the family name. Another family characteristic is a generally bright coloration, heavy on yellow and various shades of red.

The Snappers

Gray Snapper

Red Snapper

Mutton Snapper

Lane Snapper

Cubera Snapper

Dog Snapper

Schoolmaster

Yellowtail Snapper

Vermilion Snapper

Mahogany Snapper

Blackfin Snapper

Silk Snapper

Queen Snapper

Gray Snapper

Lutjanus griseus

OTHER NAMES:

Mangrove Snapper
Black Snapper
Mango
Caballerote

RANGE: *All Florida, the Bahamas and Caribbean.*

HABITAT: *Juveniles are seasonally present in nearly all shallow waters and coastal estuaries of Florida, and are plentiful throughout the year in the southern half of Florida, the Caribbean and the Bahamas. Upon reaching a size of 10 or 12 inches, nearly all Gray Snapper switch their homes to deeper waters and are fished mostly over coral reefs, artificial reefs, wrecks and Gulf ledges, although big ones can also be caught in deep channels and passes along the coast. In the Panhandle, the bigger fish of deep water are called Black Snapper.*

DESCRIPTION: Gray or greenish above and light on the underside, usually with an overall reddish hue that can range from coppery to bright brick red. Obvious black line runs from the snout through the eye to just below the dorsal fin. This line darkens when the fish feeds or gets excited.

SIZE: Few surpass 1 foot inshore, but Grays can average 2-6 pounds in deep water, and reach perhaps 20 pounds or more. World and Florida records 17 pounds.

FOOD VALUE: Excellent up to a pound or so. Large ones are stronger in taste but still very good.

GAME QUALITIES: The little fellows can be easy to catch on dead shrimp or cut bait, but as they grow they become more difficult to fool. It's generally necessary to trim down the size of hooks, leaders and terminal tackle. When hooked, Gray Snappers make strong runs, then wage a bulldogging battle all the way to boatside.

TACKLE AND BAITS: Inshore—spinning and light baitcasting rigs are best and should be baited with live shrimp, live minnows, fiddler crabs, cut shrimp, cut squid or cut baitfish. Many inshore Grays are also caught on lures, along mangrove shorelines or around snags. Surface plugs and popping flies often catch Grays, as do jigs and small shrimp flies or streamers. Offshore, heavier spinning and baitcasting tackle, and light ocean tackle, are called for. Best baits are live small fish, such as Pilchards and Sardines, live shrimp, cut squid, cut crab and cut fish.

FISHING SYSTEMS: Still Fishing; Casting; Drifting.

Red Snapper

Lutjanus campechanus

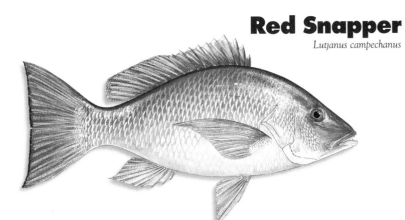

DESCRIPTION: Overall rosy red. Canine teeth less prominent than those of most other Snappers. Red eye. Anal fin is triangular. The **Caribbean Red Snapper**, *Lutjanus purpureus*, is very similar in appearance and is found in the northwest and central Caribbean.

SIZE: Common from a pound or so to about 6 or 8 pounds. Usual maximum is about 20 pounds, although the Red Snapper can rarely run as high as 30 or 40 pounds. World record 50 pounds, 4 ounces; Florida record 46 pounds, 8 ounces.

FOOD VALUE: Excellent at all sizes.

GAME QUALITIES: A hard-fighting fish that uses strong, head-shaking tactics rather than long runs.

TACKLE AND BAITS: Some Red Snapper spots in fairly shallow water, say up to 50 or 60 feet, permit the use of light ocean tackle, or even heavy spinning and baitcasting tackle. Much Snapper fishing, however—especially on long-range headboat and charterboat trips from Panhandle ports—requires deep drops in strong current. This means that only very heavy rods and strong lines of 50- or 80-pound test can handle the heavy weights needed to do the job. As for baits, dead Cigar Minnows, Pilchards or cut fish and squid do well at times, although in heavily fished spots (which most are these days) it will probably be necessary to use live small baitfish to coax bites from Snappers of decent size.

FISHING SYSTEMS: Still Fishing; Casting; Drifting.

OTHER NAMES:
North American
Red Snapper
Genuine Red
Snapper
Pargo Colorado

RANGE: *A temperate fish rather than tropical, the Red Snapper is rare in South Florida, although caught occasionally. It is standard bottom-fishing fare, however, offshore of the Atlantic Coast from about the center of the Peninsula northward, and in deep waters of the northern Gulf.*

HABITAT: *Along the Panhandle, Red Snappers are sometimes found in fairly shallow water off the beaches, and even in deep holes of the larger bays. Off the Peninsular Gulf Coast, however, few Red Snappers are found close enough to shore to merit a one-day effort; most offshore Snappers along that part of the coast are Grays.*

Mutton Snapper

Lutjanus analis

OTHER NAMES:
Muttonfish
Reef King
Pargo

RANGE: *The Mutton Snapper more or less takes over for the Red Snapper in South Florida, the Bahamas and Caribbean. On the Atlantic Coast of Florida, Muttons are common on the reefs as far north as, roughly, Fort Pierce, but gradually give way to Red Snapper after that. In the Gulf, few Muttons are caught north of the Keys, although they turn up now and then in the bags of offshore bottom fishermen all along the Gulf Coast.*

HABITAT: *Juveniles inhabit inshore grass beds, coral patches and channels. Adults are primarily inhabitants of the deeper reefs, although many are found in nearshore deep channels and passes of South Florida, the Keys and the Bahamas. Big Muttons even sneak up on certain "tailing flats" occasionally, to forage in the manner of Bonefish and Permit.*

DESCRIPTION: Coloration varies widely with size and habitat. Juveniles in shallow water are very bright, with an overall rosy appearance and mostly red fins. Adults are greenish above and red on the lower sides and underside. All sizes show blue lines in the gill cover and along the back, with a single black spot near the dorsal fin about three-quarters of the way to the fin. Vague vertical bars may be present. Anal fin is pointed.

SIZE: Inshore average is 1-2 pounds. On reefs and in deeper water, the average is 5 pounds or more, with individuals up to 15 pounds not uncommon. Maximum is probably around 35 pounds. World and Florida records 30 pounds, 4 ounces.

FOOD VALUE: Excellent.

GAME QUALITIES: Muttons are strong fighters in deep water, and can be dazzling ones in shallow water or atop the tailing flats, getting off long runs and then resisting with strength and broad sides.

TACKLE AND BAITS: For reef fishing, light ocean tackle is ideal and the best baits are live Pinfish, live Pilchards, live or cut Ballyhoo, big live shrimp and fresh cut baitfish. Light spinning or baitcasting tackle is an excellent choice inshore, when tossing jigs and plugs in channels or over grass beds and rocks. In shallow water, Muttons smash surface plugs readily. When encountered on sight-fishing flats, the same tackle is used as for Permit or Bonefish. Live crabs make the best bait here, with live shrimp also acceptable. Permit jigs and flies will also do the job, if presented well.

FISHING SYSTEMS: Still Fishing; Casting; Drifting.

Lane Snapper

Lutjanus synagris

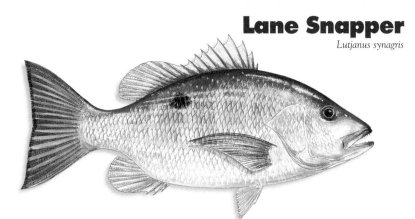

DESCRIPTION: Superficially similar to small Mutton Snapper, with which it may be confused. However, the Lane Snapper, in addition to its rosy hues, also has broken yellow bars along the sides, and its fins are mostly yellow. The single black spot on the side is larger, proportionately, than that of the Mutton. The anal fin is rounded.

SIZE: Most run well under 1 pound. Occasionally caught to 5 pounds in deep water. World record 8 pounds, 3 ounces. Florida record 6 pounds, 6 ounces.

FOOD VALUE: Very good, but flesh is soft and must be kept well iced.

GAME QUALITIES: An aggressive striker of both natural and artificial baits, the Lane is fun to catch but is not a particularly strong fighter, even for its size.

TACKLE AND BAITS: Only very light tackle provides much sport. Productive baits include live and dead shrimp and also strips of cut squid or cut fish. Small jigs worked slowly near bottom are deadly.

FISHING SYSTEMS: Still Fishing; Casting; Drifting.

OTHER NAMES:
Spot Snapper
Candy Snapper
Biajaiba

RANGE: Found off all coasts of Florida.

HABITAT: Most are caught in fairly deep reef and offshore waters, but in the southern half of the state, they also inhabit nearshore areas, and even bays. During times of warm water, they may come close to shore in the northern sectors as well. Prefers broken or grassy bottom to hard reefs.

Cubera Snapper

Lutjanus cyanopterus

OTHER NAMES:
Cuban Snapper
Cuban Dog
Snapper

RANGE: *South Florida, the Bahamas and Caribbean.*

HABITAT: *Through most of the tropics, the Cubera is at home anywhere from coastal creeks out to the deep reefs, but in Florida it is now rare to find them inshore, although one may still pop up from time to time in a creek or canal of South Florida and the Keys. Creeks of the larger Bahamas Out Islands also harbor a few of them. Most are caught around wrecks and reef dropoffs in 100-200 feet of water off Dade County and Key Largo, but they may surprise anglers at times in offshore waters anywhere from the Dry Tortugas to about halfway up the Florida Peninsula.*

DESCRIPTION: The Cubera looks like a gigantic Gray Snapper and, in fact, oversize Grays—those longer than a couple feet—are almost always confused with smallish Cuberas. To really tell the difference you have to check the patch of vomerine teeth on the inside roof of the mouth. In the Gray, this patch is shaped something like an arrow, complete with shaft. That of the Cubera is of similar shape but has no shaft; it looks like an inverted "V".

SIZE: The giant among Snappers, Cuberas often reach or exceed 100 pounds, and the average is 30-50 pounds. World record 121 pounds, 8 ounces; Florida record 116 pounds.

FOOD VALUE: Excellent to about 40 pounds. Larger ones tend to coarseness, and carry the possibility of causing Ciguatera poisoning (see Introduction).

GAME QUALITIES: A real brawler that uses its size, strength and every obstacle in the vicinity to great advantage.

TACKLE AND BAITS: Realistically, ocean gear with lines testing upward of 50 pounds should be used for Cubera fishing, even though quite a few big ones have been caught on lighter lines—and occasionally even on heavy spinning and plug tackle by deep-jigging anglers. Most Cuberas caught by design are taken at night off North Key Largo and South Dade during the summer months. By far the best bait is a whole live lobster. Whole live blue crabs make a fair substitute, as do live Blue Runner and similar baitfish. Cuberas are perfectly willing to take dead baits too, but usually get beaten to them by smaller fish.

FISHING SYSTEMS: Drifting; Still Fishing.

Dog Snapper

Lutjanus jocu

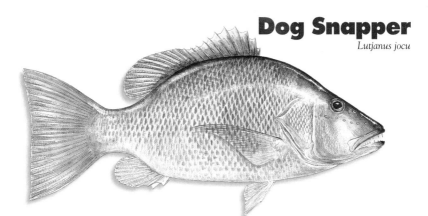

DESCRIPTION: The name comes, of course, from the canine teeth, which seem even more prominent than in most other large Snappers. Overall coloration is light orange or yellowish, darker on the back and lighter on the sides. The tail and dorsal fin are deep yellow or orange, while the other fins are lighter yellow. There is a broken blue streak on gill cover below the eye and a white, V-shaped patch on the gill cover, under the blue markings.

SIZE: Although most catches run only a couple of pounds, the Dog Snapper is not uncommon at 10 or 15 pounds and can reach 30 or more. World record 24 pounds.

FOOD VALUE: Excellent in all sizes.

GAME QUALITIES: A strong fighter.

TACKLE AND BAITS: Offshore, Dog Snappers are less common than Gray Snappers but are taken on the same tackle and baits—usually light to medium ocean-fishing outfits with lines to 30-pound test. Best baits are live baitfish and cut Ballyhoo or squid.

FISHING SYSTEMS: Still Fishing; Drifting.

OTHER NAMES:

Yellow Snapper
Jocu

RANGE: *Most of Florida plus Bahamas and Caribbean.*

HABITAT: *Adults mostly prowl the coral reefs of South Florida, the Keys and Bahamas. Elsewhere, it is occasionally caught offshore. Juveniles live in shallow rocky areas of tropical shoals and shorelines.*

Schoolmaster

Lutjanus apodus

OTHER NAMES:

Barred Snapper
Caji

RANGE: All Florida, the Bahamas and Caribbean.

HABITAT: Juveniles are plentiful in shallow coastal waters; as they grow, they work into deeper and deeper water. Dense schools are often encountered by divers over shallow wrecks and certain coral patches—making the name derivation obvious. Biggest Schoolmasters stick to reefs and dropoffs in deep water.

DESCRIPTION: Deep-bodied and overall yellowish, with several prominent vertical white bars on the sides. In the largest specimens, these bars may be nearly invisible, and so lead to confusion with the Dog Snapper. Another similarity is that both have a blue line, usually broken, on the gill cover. The Schoolmaster, however, does not have the white cone-shaped patch on the gill that identifies the Dog Snapper. Since most Schoolmasters are rather small and vividly striped, their identity is pretty obvious.

SIZE: Averages a pound or less in shallow water. Big individuals on the deep reefs may reach 6 or 7 pounds. World and Florida records 13 pounds, 4 ounces.

FOOD VALUE: Excellent.

GAME QUALITIES: Equivalent to other Snappers of similar size.

TACKLE AND BAITS: Light spinning and baitcasting outfits. Live or dead shrimp, squid and small fish are all acceptable baits. Schoolmasters will take small jigs on occasion but are seldom enthusiastic about them.

FISHING SYSTEMS: Still Fishing; Drifting.

Yellowtail Snapper

Ocyurus chrysurus

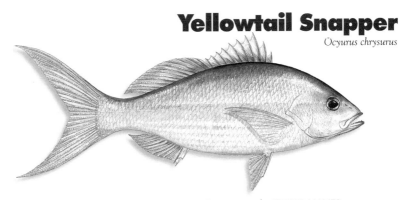

DESCRIPTION: Identified by a yellow stripe that runs the full length of the body from forward of the eye to the deeply forked yellow tail. The stripe is vivid in young fish, but pales with maturity. Color above the line is bluish with yellow patches; silvery white below. No prominent teeth as in most other Snappers.

SIZE: From less than a foot in coastal shallows to an average of 1-3 pounds on deep reefs. "Flags" running as heavy as 4 or 5 pounds are common, and a few run to 7 or 8 pounds. World record 11 pounds; Florida record 8 pounds, 9 ounces.

FOOD VALUE: Excellent if fresh or well-iced.

GAME QUALITIES: Pound-for-pound, among the best of reef fishes. Because most are hooked high in the water column, they usually make long, strong runs. Yellowtail are masters at cutting lines on the edge of a dropoff, or fouling them on high reef growth.

TACKLE AND BAITS: Undersize fish in the shallows will greedily hit nearly any bait or lure. Yellowtails of decent size, however, are almost always caught in outside reef areas. They are among the wariest of biters, generally requiring lighter lines, leaders, hooks and sinkers than the angler would really like to use. Regulars mostly try to get by with spinning tackle and 15-pound line, but on many days must go to 12-pound lines or smaller, to produce or sustain any action. Small dead baits—cut fish, cut squid and pieces of shrimp catch the most Yellowtails because those baits are similar in size and buoyancy to the ground chum that is used to lure them close and turn on their appetites. In many areas of the Bahamas and Caribbean, Yellowtail are caught by trolling a variety of lures, or by casting with small jigs, and even flies. Best luck anywhere is likely to come at night.

FISHING SYSTEMS: Still Fishing; Drifting; Trolling.

OTHER NAMES:
Flag
Tail
Rabirubia

RANGE: *Yellowtail are common only in South Florida, the Bahamas and the Caribbean, although odd catches are made in other areas of the state, especially offshore Gulf reefs.*

HABITAT: *Small fish grow up around shallow coastal reefs and patches. Best fishing depths in most areas are 60 to about 120 feet, with nearly all the "Flags" coming from the deepest habitat. Yellowtail school heavily and hang around dropoffs or humps.*

Vermilion Snapper

Rhomboplites aurorubens

OTHER NAMES:
Beeliner
Mingo
Cajon

RANGE: *All Florida coasts; more common northward.*

HABITAT: *Prefers the same depths as the Red Snapper, with which it often mixes. A common panfish around offshore deep wrecks, reefs and ledges of the upper Atlantic and Gulf Coasts. Like the Red Snapper, it is more of a temperate than a tropical fish, and is unfamiliar to most anglers in the southern reaches of the state.*

DESCRIPTION: Rosy red above, fading to pinkish then whitish below. Red fins. Large eye. Similar to the Red Snapper in color but easily distinguished in addition to much smaller average size by the lack of prominent "snapper teeth", and by its rounded anal fin.

SIZE: Averages less than a pound. May rarely reach 5 pounds or slightly larger. World record 7 pounds, 3 ounces.

FOOD VALUE: An excellent panfish.

GAME QUALITIES: Poor. Most are caught on too-heavy tackle at considerable depth—not a sporting combination for a small fish.

TACKLE AND BAITS: Since the Vermilion is caught in greatest quantity by partyboat fishermen, the usual tackle consists of rods and reels stout enough to handle the hoped-for Snapper and Grouper. Even if the fisherman specifically targets Vermilions, he generally has to use the same tackle and heavy sinkers, switching only to smaller hooks. When conditions are favorable enough to permit getting down with weights of an ounce or so, spinning and baitcasting tackle are more productive—and certainly more fun. Beeliners usually bite greedily at any sort of small dead bait, including cut fish, squid and shrimp.

FISHING SYSTEMS: Still Fishing; Drifting.

Mahogany Snapper
Lutjanus mahogoni

DESCRIPTION: Brightly colored, but with little of the reds and pinks that characterize most tropical Snappers. Back and upper sides are tan to deep brown. The underside is silvery. Dark spot on lateral line below posterior dorsal fin. Eye large.

SIZE: To perhaps 3 pounds.

FOOD VALUE: Excellent.

GAME QUALITIES: Good as other small Snappers.

TACKLE AND BAITS: Spinning, baitcasting and light ocean outfits with small hooks and sinkers and cut bait. This is an odd catch that crops up now and then among mixed bags of small reef fish.

FISHING SYSTEMS: Still Fishing.

OTHER NAMES:
Ojonco

RANGE: South Florida, the Bahamas and Caribbean.

HABITAT: Tropical reefs, although not common anywhere. Occasionally caught in the Keys, but more are seen in the Bahamas.

Blackfin Snapper
Lutjanus buccanella

DESCRIPTION: Vivid red overall, with black crescent-shaped mark at base of the pectoral fin.

SIZE: Averages 3 or 4 pounds; usual maximum is 10 or so. World record 7 pounds, 3 ounces.

FOOD VALUE: Excellent.

GAME QUALITIES: Strong fighter like other Snappers.

TACKLE AND BAITS: Blackfin Snapper generally stay well beyond the depths of anchoring. Most are caught while drifting and jigging off cliffs and ledges. Blackfins eagerly strike a heavy bucktail or nylon jig.

FISHING SYSTEMS: Drifting.

OTHER NAMES:
Blackspot Snapper
Bahamas Red Snapper

RANGE: South Florida, the Bahamas and Caribbean.

HABITAT: Nearly all are caught along outside dropoffs at depths of 200 feet or greater. Most are caught in the Bahamas.

Silk Snapper

Lutjanus vivanus

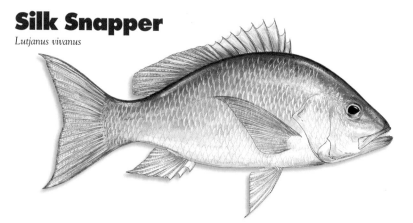

OTHER NAMES:
Yelloweye

RANGE: *All Florida, the Bahamas and Caribbean.*

HABITAT: *These are deep-ocean Snappers that are seldom caught any shallower than 300 or 400 feet, and are common at 100 fathoms and deeper.*

DESCRIPTION: The Silk Snapper is pink overall and is shaped much like the Red Snapper, although the yellow eye distinguishes it. The pectorals are pale yellow and the back portion of the caudal fin has a black edge.

SIZE: Averages 3 to 5 pounds. Maximum sizes uncertain. World record 18 pounds, 5 ounces.

FOOD VALUE: Excellent; probably the best of all the Snappers. In general, however, it can be observed that all the edible species of fish hauled up from great depths make exceptionally fine table fare.

GAME QUALITIES: No battle can be expected, thanks to the great depth and the non-sporting gear required.

TACKLE AND BAITS: Anglers are unlikely to encounter this fish unless they fish very deep with several pounds of lead, stout rods and electric reels—for meat or curiosity, rather than sport. Commercial fishermen pull them up with motorized winches. Any sort of cut bait can be used.

FISHING SYSTEMS: Specialized deep systems only.

Queen Snapper

Etelis oculatus

DESCRIPTION: The Queen Snapper is bright red on its upper and lower sides, and shaped more like the Yellowtail. It has silvery sides and a deeply forked red tail that continues to lengthen as the fish grows. The eye is very large and yellow.

SIZE: Averages 3 to 5 pounds. Maximum sizes uncertain. World record 11 pounds, 11 ounces.

FOOD VALUE: Excellent; probably one of the best of all the Snappers, although the same can be said of other Snappers that come from the deepest habitats.

GAME QUALITIES: No battle can be expected, thanks to the great depth and the non-sporting gear required.

TACKLE AND BAITS: As with other deepwater Snappers, the Queen isn't seen by anglers unless they're using lots of lead and hefty gear. Any type of cut bait can be used.

FISHING SYSTEMS: Specialized deep systems only.

RANGE: All Florida, the Bahamas and Caribbean.

HABITAT: This is another deep-ocean Snapper that is seldom caught any shallower than 300 or 400 feet, and is probably most common at 600 feet and deeper.

Along all coasts of Florida and the Bahamas, from inshore cuts and holes out to the deepest water fishable by hook and line, Groupers of various sorts are among the most popular and widely available of gamefish. Their great variety is seen not only in the sheer number of species, but also in the many different approaches taken in fishing for them, and the seemingly endless array of baits and lures that are productive.

Although they rank as the No. 1 pets of offshore bottom fishermen, huge numbers of Grouper are also caught by casters and trollers. In many situations, they even respond well to fly casting. All Groupers belong to the same family, Serranidae, but can be divided into two broad categories that are identifiable by general appearance. Those belonging to the genus Epinephelus—typified by the Goliath and Red Grouper—are chunky and deep-bodied, whereas those belonging to the genus Mycteroperca—typified by the Gag and Black Groupers—are considerably more streamlined. Mycteroperca Groupers—at least the very large specimens—are more often implicated in Ciguatera poisoning (see Introduction) than the Epinephelus group. But all this need not cause Florida anglers any great concern, since most catches are of small to medium fish.

The Groupers

Gag

Black Grouper

Yellowfin Grouper

Scamp

Yellowmouth Grouper

Tiger Grouper

Goliath Grouper

Warsaw Grouper

Red Grouper

Nassau Grouper

Red Hind

Rock Hind

Coney

Graysby

Speckled Hind

Marbled Grouper

Misty Grouper

Snowy Grouper

Yellowedge Grouper

Black Sea Bass

Sand Perch

Gag
Mycteroperca microlepis

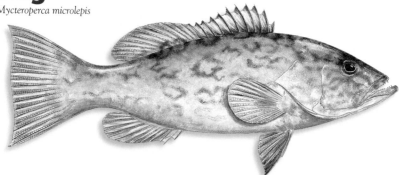

OTHER NAMES:

Gray Grouper
Grass Grouper
Copper Belly
Black Grouper

RANGE: *Found throughout Florida and Bahamas.*

HABITAT: *Both juveniles and adults frequent inshore holes and ledges, often on deeper grass flats. From there they can be found around structure at virtually any fishable offshore depth.*

DESCRIPTION: Gray or light brown with wavy markings on the side that generally do not form boxes or circles. Edges of fins are bluish. Color deepens to dark brown shortly after removal from water.

SIZE: Can reach 50 pounds on deep offshore wrecks and ledges, and has been recorded to 80 pounds, but 20-30 is the usual maximum range, and most catches now fall between 2 and 12 pounds. Many juveniles are caught from inshore grass flats. World record 80 pounds, 6 ounces; Florida record 80 pounds, 6 ounces.

FOOD VALUE: Excellent; firm white flesh; little red.

GAME QUALITIES: An aggressive striker and hard fighter at all depths.

TACKLE AND BAITS: Just about anything goes. Offshore bottom fishermen tend toward stout rods with 50- and 80-pound-test lines, but such "grouper digging" rigs are strictly necessary only in very deep water. Up to about 50 feet, lines in the 20-30-pound range are adequate and allow much more sport. Many anglers catch lots of Gags on spinning and plug tackle. This is also the best of the Groupers for fly fishermen, since they are frequently found in fairly shallow water and will eagerly take a large streamer fly. Hard-lure casters use leadhead jigs, mostly, while trollers rely on large deep-diving plugs. Live baitfish of various sorts are the best natural offerings—try Pilchards, Pinfish, Grunts or Sand Perch (Squirrelfish). Dead small fish and large cut baits also work well.

FISHING SYSTEMS: Still Fishing; Drifting; Trolling.

Black Grouper

Mycteroperca bonaci

DESCRIPTION: Overall color is dark gray. Markings are blacker than those of the Gag, and form box-like patterns. Fins are black; their edges also black or deep blue.

SIZE: The largest of our *Mycteroperca* groupers, the Black frequently exceeds 50 pounds in weight and can top 100 pounds. World record 124 pounds.

FOOD VALUE: Excellent.

GAME QUALITIES: Considered best of the Groupers.

TACKLE AND BAITS: For all-around work, ocean gear with lines of 30-pound test or higher gets the call. Light-tackle fishermen in South Florida, however, have caught many Blacks over 50 pounds. One key—besides a huge helping of luck—is to hook the fish while drifting, instead of at anchor. The drift of the boat adds to the power of the tackle and just might help drag the big fish far enough away from his rocky "hole" that he cannot get back. For drifting or still fishing, the best baits are frisky live fish, such as Blue Runners or other small jacks. Pinfish and Pilchards are good too, as are Mullet heads and other large cut baits. Best casting lures are leadhead jigs, weighing from 1-4 ounces, depending on depth. Trolling over the reefs with rigged, swimming Mullet, feather-and-strip combos, and large plugs also takes many.

FISHING SYSTEMS: Drifting; Still Fishing; Trolling.

OTHER NAMES:
Bonaci Arara
Aguaji

RANGE: Sometimes encountered in the deep Gulf and upper Atlantic, but common only in South Florida, the Keys and the Bahamas.

HABITAT: Blacks of many sizes are commonly found around the edges of coral reefs, from about 30 feet of water out to the deepest dropoffs. Even big fish, however, may roam to much shallower patch reefs, especially in cooler seasons. Small Blacks may also frequent creeks, especially in the Bahamas.

Yellowfin Grouper

Mycteroperca venenosa

OTHER NAMES:

Red Rockfish
Spotted Grouper
Bonaci Cardinal

RANGE: *Roughly the same as the Black Grouper; it is most common in the Bahamas.*

HABITAT: *Again, its preferred reef habitat is pretty much the same as that of the Black Grouper.*

DESCRIPTION: Shows various colors, including two major phases, one of which would make it difficult to tell from the Black Grouper were it not for the bright yellow trim of the pectoral fins. In its other major color phase, the Yellowfin is the prettiest of all the Groupers—overall bright red with dark red or brown box-shaped blotches and, of course, the yellow pectorals. In both phases, yellow may be obvious on other fins, as well as the pectorals.

SIZE: This is a good-size Grouper that frequently runs to 15 pounds or so, and sometimes to 30 or more. The smaller ones, from 3-10 pounds, are apt to be the most brightly colored. World record 40 pounds, 12 ounces; Florida record 34 pounds, 6 ounces.

FOOD VALUE: Smaller fish are excellent. So are the big fellows—but see the comments about Ciguatera in the Introduction.

GAME QUALITIES: Outstanding; among the best of the groupers.

TACKLE AND BAITS: Almost anything goes, from heavy bottom-fishing outfits to the rather beefy spinning and baitcasting outfits that are used for jigging. Although live baits will take the most Yellowfins, large cut baits also work pretty well. Many are caught by trolling, especially with heavy feather-and-strip combinations. They also take plugs and spoons.

FISHING SYSTEMS: Still Fishing; Drifting; Trolling.

Scamp

Mycteroperca phenax

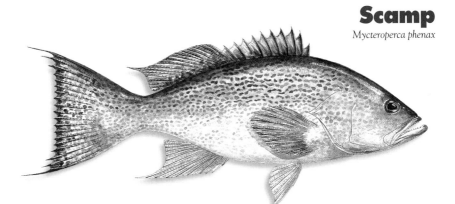

DESCRIPTION: Overall coloration is a deep tan or chocolate brown, with numerous darker markings that form dots, or lines, or groups of lines. Elongated rays of the caudal fin give the broomtail appearance.

SIZE: Usually well under 10 pounds, but occasionally more than 20. World record 29 pounds, 10 ounces; Florida record 28 pounds, 6 ounces.

FOOD VALUE: Excellent. Commercially considered as the prize of all the Groupers.

GAME QUALITIES: Outstanding on light tackle, but most are overpowered by heavy gear.

TACKLE AND BAITS: Sheer depth—typical of many Panhandle bottom-fishing drops—may necessitate rods and lines stout enough to handle very heavy sinkers. In depths where practical, however, spinning and baitcasting tackle will handle Scamps admirably— and provide great sport as well as a great dinner. Leadhead jigs weighing 3/4 of an ounce to 1½ ounces get lots of strikes with light gear—and if the bare jig isn't producing, it can be tipped with a strip of cut bait, or a whole small baitfish, and used as a bottom-fishing rig. Any kind of small fish makes a fine live bait. Shrimp, squid and cut baits also do the job. Large diving plugs draw strikes in fairly shallow water—to about 50 feet.

FISHING SYSTEMS: Still Fishing; Drifting; Trolling.

OTHER NAMES:

Brown Grouper
Broomtail Grouper
Abadejo

RANGE: *Most plentiful along the Gulf Coast and roughly the upper half of the Florida Atlantic Coast. Not common in South Florida and the Bahamas, where it is largely replaced by the similar Yellowmouth Grouper (next).*

HABITAT: *Sometimes fairly close to shore, but generally sticks to deep reefs and ledges offshore.*

Yellowmouth Grouper

Mycteroperca interstitialis

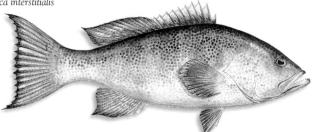

OTHER NAMES:
Salmon Rockfish

RANGE: *Most common in the Bahamas but found in South Florida, especially the Keys, and on Gulf reefs.*

HABITAT: *Occasionally on shallow patches, but more on deeper reefs—to 120 feet or so—near the edge of blue water.*

DESCRIPTION: Almost a ringer for the Scamp, except that the inside and corners of the mouth are yellow.

SIZE: Averages 2-3 pounds; maximum probably less than 10 pounds. World record 13 pounds.

FOOD VALUE: Excellent.

GAME QUALITIES: A tough fighter on tackle of reasonable size.

TACKLE AND BAITS: Same as Scamp.

FISHING SYSTEMS: Still Fishing; Trolling; Drifting.

Tiger Grouper

Mycteroperca tigris

OTHER NAMES:
Bonaci Gato

RANGE: *More common in the Bahamas, but seen fairly often in the Keys. Rare elsewhere in Florida.*

HABITAT: *Coral reefs.*

DESCRIPTION: Dark markings against a dusty gray background form vivid oblique stripes on the upper sides. Smaller wormlike markings on lower sides and fins.

SIZE: A medium-size Grouper, averaging under 10 pounds. World record 14 pounds, 8 ounces.

FOOD VALUE: Excellent.

GAME QUALITIES: Equal to Groupers of similar size.

TACKLE AND BAITS: Heavy spinning and baitcasting outfits, along with light boat rods and lines up to 20- or 30-pound test. Best baits are small live fish and fresh cut fish or squid. Tigers will take a variety of artificials, including jigs and trolling plugs.

FISHING SYSTEMS: Still Fishing; Drifting; Trolling.

Goliath Grouper

Epinephelus itajara

DESCRIPTION: This is by far the largest of the Groupers, but at any size, there's no mistaking a Goliath Grouper. Juveniles are brilliantly marked with a series of irregular dark brown bars against a light brown or gray background, extending from head to tail. Numerous black spots are usually present as well on head, sides and fins. Adults have the same pattern but in more subdued shades of brown that are not so brilliantly contrasted. The tail is round, as are the posterior, dorsal, anal and pectoral fins.

SIZE: Traditionally seen in many sizes from a few pounds to 500 pounds. Reported to reach half a ton. The really huge fish are rare anymore, but slowly returning. World and Florida records 680 pounds.

FOOD VALUE: Small ones excellent and big ones darn good—which was the main reason for their precipitous decline and total closure in Florida in the 1980s.

GAME QUALITIES: Inshore juveniles are great battlers. Some very big ones have been caught on very light lines in shallow water—after being coaxed away from obstructions, but the giant Goliath around deep wrecks defy the heaviest sporting tackle.

TACKLE AND BAITS: Baitcasting, spinning and even fly tackle make acceptable matchups for the inshore fish, which will—and often do—hit the full range of lures and flies that are used by Snook casters. Again, though, it takes all the muscle you and your tackle can come up with to battle Goliath of 100 pounds or more. Best natural baits are live Snapper, live Jack and live Catfish inshore; live or dead large fish for offshore giants—including Bonito and Amberjack up to 15 pounds or more.

FISHING SYSTEMS: Still Fishing; Drift Fishing.

OTHER NAMES:
Jewfish
Spotted Jewfish
Great Grouper
Guasa Mero

RANGE: Occurs throughout Florida and the Bahamas.

HABITAT: Juveniles to around 100 pounds frequent mangrove creeks and bays of Southwest Florida, especially the Ten Thousand Islands and Everglades National Park. Adults can be found at a variety of depths, from holes and channels of coastal waters out to offshore ledges and reefs; also around pilings of bridges and under deepwater docks and piers.

Warsaw Grouper

Epinephelus nigritus

OTHER NAMES:

Giant Grouper
Black Jewfish
Garrupa Negrita

RANGE: *All Florida coasts, Atlantic and Gulf, but not reported from the Bahamas.*

HABITAT: *Very deep dropoffs, ledges and seamounts. Seldom encountered in less than 200 feet, and most common in much deeper water. Partyboats working offshore waters of the state's upper half–both Gulf and Atlantic–seem to bring in Warsaws more often than elsewhere.*

DESCRIPTION: Mottled dark brown, shading to slightly lighter brown on lower portions. Tail square and yellowish. Second dorsal spine is elongated and crestlike.

SIZE: This is the second-largest Grouper, commonly caught at 30-80 pounds, with 100-pounders not rare. Probably grows to more than 500. World and Florida records 436 pounds, 12 ounces.

FOOD VALUE: Good. Large specimens (which most are) can be somewhat coarse unless the fillets are cut into thin steaks for frying or baking.

GAME QUALITIES: Great strength is the hallmark of the Warsaw's fighting arsenal, and the angler who gets one on a manual rod and reel will know he's been in a tug-of-war.

TACKLE AND BAITS: Only the heaviest rods, large reels and lines testing 80 pounds or more are really adequate. Catches on lighter tackle are opportunistic and rare, and usually of the smaller specimens. Fairly large whole fish, or halved bonito and other hefty cut baits are all productive whenever they can be dropped to within gulping range of a Warsaw.

FISHING SYSTEMS: Still Fishing; Drifting.

Red Grouper

Epinephelus morio

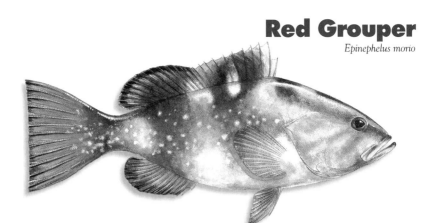

DESCRIPTION: Overall light or rusty red with whitish spots and large blotches. No black mark on caudal peduncle fleshy area between tail and posterior dorsal fin.

SIZE: Common at 1-10 pounds; maximum perhaps 40 pounds. World record 42 pounds, 4 ounces; Florida record 42 pounds, 4 ounces.

FOOD VALUE: Good.

GAME QUALITIES: One of the toughest-fighting Groupers, pound-for-pound. Although Reds will "hole up" like other Groupers, many are hooked on light and fairly light tackle in areas where cover is well scattered, and this gives them the chance to demonstrate their toughness to best advantage.

TACKLE AND BAITS: The standard tackle is a boat outfit with 40-pound line or more, but heavy spinning and baitcasting tackle with 15- or 20-pound line can easily do the job in water less than 100 feet deep. Reds will hit all the baits and lures recommended for Gag and other Groupers, but they are also very fond of crustacean baits, particularly shrimp and crab. They are ready strikers on leadhead jigs, fished with light tackle.

FISHING SYSTEMS: Still Fishing; Drifting; Trolling.

OTHER NAMES:
Mero
Cherna De Vivero

RANGE: *Common throughout Florida; also present in Bahamas and common in some areas.*

HABITAT: *Widely distributed from close inshore in many areas of Florida to ledges and wrecks in up to 300 or so feet of water. Great majority of sport catches are made in 10-100 feet.*

Nassau Grouper

Epinephelus striatus

OTHER NAMES:
White Grouper
Bahamas Grouper
Rockfish
Cherna Criolla

RANGE: *Occurs throughout the Caribbean and Bahamas, where it is the best known of the Groupers. Also found in Southeast Florida and the Keys, where it is rare and declining.*

HABITAT: *Prefers coral reefs, and probably does not roam into water much deeper than 120 feet or so. In the Islands, small specimens are common over inshore patches, and also in creeks and channels.*

DESCRIPTION: Looks much like the Red Grouper in shape and pattern, although the basic coloration tends more to brown or gray than reddish. The sure distinguishing feature is a black blotch on the caudal peduncle.

SIZE: Common at 1-10 pounds. May reach 30 or more. World record 38 pounds, 8 ounces; Florida record 3 pounds, 4 ounces.

FOOD VALUE: Small ones are excellent; fish over 10 pounds are almost as good, but harvest is currently prohibited in Florida.

GAME QUALITIES: A rugged fighter.

TACKLE AND BAITS: Most are caught by potluck reef or creek fishermen on light ocean gear or stout bait-casting and spinning outfits—all using lines of 12-20 pounds. Cut fish, conch or squid all make good baits, and Nassau's will also strike jigs, spoons and underwater or surface plugs. Bigger fish on rough coral reefs require heavy tackle for bottom-fishing, and can also be caught by trolling with feather-and-strip baits or with large swimming plugs.

FISHING SYSTEMS: Still Fishing; Trolling; Drifting.

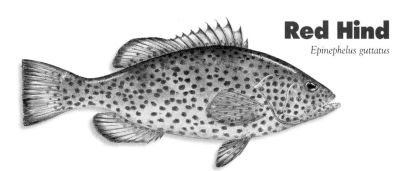

Red Hind
Epinephelus guttatus

DESCRIPTION: Numerous bright red spots on lighter or creamy red background. Caudal, anal and posterior dorsal fins edged in black.

SIZE: Most run 1-2 pounds; rarely 5-6 pounds. World record 8 pounds, 7 ounces.

FOOD VALUE: Excellent.

GAME QUALITIES: Aggressive striker; lethargic battler.

TACKLE AND BAITS: In some reef areas of the Bahamas, Red Hinds can be caught to the point of boredom by drifting and bouncing the bottom with jigs. Bottom fishing with cut baits of any kind is also productive.

FISHING SYSTEMS: Drifting; Still Fishing.

OTHER NAMES:
Strawberry
Sandwich Grouper
Cabrilla
Tofia

RANGE: *Very plentiful on Bahamas reefs in 40-80 feet. Also found in South Florida, but less common and usually in 100 feet or more.*

HABITAT: *Coral reefs.*

Rock Hind
Epinephelus adscensionis

DESCRIPTION: The Rock Hind is mostly brown or tan in background color. Has spots similar to those of the Red Hind, but also is marked by large, dark blotches on the upper sides—usually two, but often more.

SIZE: About the same as the Red Hind, but maximum may be slightly larger—to 8 or 9 pounds. World record 9 pounds.

FOOD VALUE: Excellent.

GAME QUALITIES: Same as Red Hind.

TACKLE AND BAITS: Same as Red Hind.

FISHING SYSTEMS: Drifting; Still Fishing.

OTHER NAMES:
Rock Cod
Cabre Mora
Mero Cabrilla

RANGE: *Widespread in Florida and the Bahamas, often in company with the Red Hind, but usually less plentiful in southern portions of the range.*

HABITAT: *Coral reefs and rocky banks.*

Coney

Epinephelus fulvus

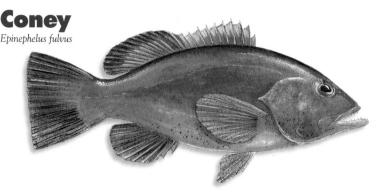

OTHER NAMES:

Golden Coney
Golden Grouper
Guativere
Corruncha

RANGE: South Florida, Bahamas and Caribbean.

HABITAT: Coral reefs and inshore coral patches.

DESCRIPTION: A very small Grouper, the Coney is seen in various color phases, including vivid yellow, gold-and-brown, red-and-brown.

SIZE: Most run 6-8 inches; maximum maybe a foot.

FOOD VALUE: Not much to work with.

GAME QUALITIES: Aggressive striker, but small.

TACKLE AND BAITS: Never targeted. If it were, only ultralight would be chosen. Takes a variety of cut baits, plus jigs.

FISHING SYSTEMS: Still Fishing.

Graysby

Epinephelus cruentatus

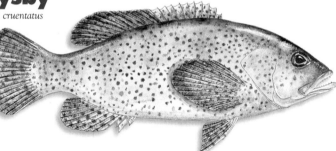

OTHER NAMES:

Enjambre
Cuna Cabrilla

RANGE: South Florida, Bahamas and Caribbean.

HABITAT: Coral reefs and patches.

DESCRIPTION: Usually gray with many tiny, dark dots. Series of four spots below dorsal fin.

SIZE: Under 1 foot. World record 2 pounds, 8 ounces.

FOOD VALUE: Small.

GAME QUALITIES: Aggressive striker, sometimes on surprisingly large lures, but too small to put up a fight.

TACKLE AND BAITS: Like the Coney, a common reef catch when small hooks are used. Takes any small cut bait or jig.

FISHING SYSTEMS: Still Fishing.

Speckled Hind

Epinephelus drummondhayi

DESCRIPTION: Generally dark gray or reddish brown, with a profusion of small, creamy or white spots on sides, gill covers and fins. Sometimes light tan or yellow with whiter spots.

SIZE: Can run to 40 pounds or more; most catches range from 5 to 20 pounds. World record 52 pounds, 8 ounces; Florida record 52 pounds, 8 ounces.

FOOD VALUE: This and other deepwater species that follow are considered even better table fare than shallow-water species. The same is true of deep-sea Snappers and Porgies. It is theorized that the great pressures under which they live helps make the flesh more succulent.

GAME QUALITIES: Seldom caught on sporting gear, but when they are—especially if that gear is a reasonably light outfit, the fight begins strong but diminishes fast as the fish is brought higher in the water column. This, of course, is typical with any sort of Grouper that is hooked at depth. Somewhere along the way, the pressure changes enough to send them bobbing upward.

TACKLE AND BAITS: Electric reels and wire line. Catches on sporting tackle are seldom made by design. Any kind of cut bait seems to work well.

FISHING SYSTEMS: Still Fishing; Drifting.

OTHER NAMES:

Kitty Mitchell
Calico Grouper

RANGE: *Both coasts of Florida, but most often caught in the Keys—and this is probably because of heavy fishing around well-known seamounts or "humps," particularly off the Keys towns of Marathon and Islamorada.*

HABITAT: *An occasional small specimen is caught by bottom-fishing in perhaps 200 feet of water in the Keys, but most stick to ledges and outcroppings at least 300 feet down. They are probably plentiful in much deeper water.*

Marbled Grouper

Epinephelus inermis

RANGE: Bahamas and South Florida.

HABITAT: Very deep dropoffs or seamounts in 500 feet or more of water.

DESCRIPTION: Dark brown or charcoal with numerous white spots. Deeper-bodied than most Groupers, its shape is reminiscent of the unrelated Tripletail.

SIZE: Averages 5-10 pounds; sometimes exceeds 20. World record 10 pounds; 8 ounces.

FOOD VALUE: Excellent, as are all the Groupers that inhabit very deep water.

GAME QUALITIES: Seldom caught on sporting gear.

TACKLE AND BAITS: Power reels and cut baitfish or squid.

FISHING SYSTEMS: Drifting.

Misty Grouper

Epinephelus mystacinus

OTHER NAMES:

Mystic Grouper
Mustache Grouper

RANGE: The Bahamas and extreme South Florida.

HABITAT: Rocks and ledges in 500 feet or more.

DESCRIPTION: Brown with 6 to 9 vertical whitish bars.

SIZE: Common at 15-50 pounds; exceeds 100 pounds.

FOOD VALUE: Excellent.

GAME QUALITIES: Seldom caught on sporting gear.

TACKLE AND BAITS: Power reels with cut bait.

FISHING SYSTEMS: Drifting.

Snowy Grouper

Epinephelus niveatus

DESCRIPTION: Dark gray or brown with scattered whitish spots.

SIZE: Averages 5-10 pounds; said to reach 50 pounds. World and Florida records 37 pounds, 9 ounces.

FOOD VALUE: Excellent.

GAME QUALITIES: Not caught on sporting tackle.

TACKLE AND BAITS: Power reels; cut baits.

FISHING SYSTEMS: Drifting.

OTHER NAMES:

Golden Grouper

RANGE: *Occurs in deep water throughout Florida and the Western Bahamas; probably Eastern Bahamas as well.*

HABITAT: *Small ones may come in as shallow as 250 or 300 feet on occasion, but most stick to 600-1,000 feet.*

Yellowedge Grouper

Epinephelus flavolimbatus

DESCRIPTION: Mottled light brown overall. Dorsal, pectoral and anal fins have yellow outer edges.

SIZE: Averages 5 or 10 pounds; may exceed 30 pounds. World and Florida records 41 pounds, 1 ounce.

FOOD VALUE: Excellent.

GAME QUALITIES: Seldom caught on sporting tackle.

TACKLE AND BAITS: Power reels best. Heaviest manual rods and reels possible. Any kind of cut bait.

FISHING SYSTEMS: Drifting.

OTHER NAMES:
Deepwater
Yellowfin
Grouper

RANGE: *All Florida and the Bahamas.*

HABITAT: *Not quite so deep as three preceding species. Over deep coral reefs at times, but prefers 300 feet and more.*

Black Sea Bass

Centropristis striata

OTHER NAMES:

Sea Bass
Black Bass
Blackfish
Rockfish
Talywag

RANGE: *A temperate fish, it is most common off Central and North Florida. Straggles to South Florida, but is absent from the Bahamas.*

HABITAT: *Widely at home, both offshore and inshore. Likes rocky areas, wrecks, channels with hard bottom, jetties, deep holes in grass flats. Larger fish now stay mostly well offshore.*

DESCRIPTION: Color is generally black or charcoal, with blue highlights and tiny white spots or stripes on dorsal fin. Indistinct pattern sometimes present on sides, especially in small fish. In adults, the dorsal, anal and caudal fins may have feathery edges, and large males show a distinctive hump forward of the dorsal.

SIZE: Recorded to at least 8 pounds, but individuals weighing more than one pound are now rather uncommon, and a 3- or 4-pounder is a rare giant. World record 10 pounds, 4 ounces; Florida record 5 pounds, 1 ounce.

FOOD VALUE: Excellent. The flesh is mild and white but, sadly, most Sea Bass caught these days are too small to be worthwhile. The occasional outsize specimen should be filleted and skinned, but take care when doing so, because gill covers are sharp and so are the spines.

GAME QUALITIES: A hard and willing striker on both natural baits and a variety of artificial lures. Pulls hard for its size, but is too often caught on too-heavy tackle.

TACKLE AND BAITS: Light spinning and baitcasting tackle are the best choices. Sea Bass greedily hit live or dead shrimp and all sorts of cut baits, along with live small baitfish and artificial jigs and underwater plugs. They seem to be always hungry and willing to strike nearly anything they can grab.

FISHING SYSTEMS: Still Fishing; Casting; Trolling; Drifting.

Sand Perch

Diplectrum formosum

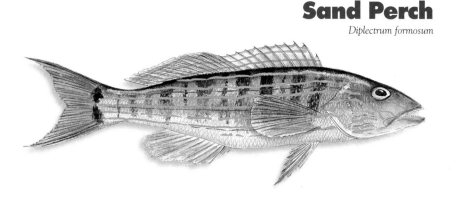

DESCRIPTION: Slender, cylindrical shape, with large mouth and wide tail. Color is tan with brown vertical bars or blotches, and full-length horizontal lines of blue and orange.

SIZE: Less than a foot; average is 6-8 inches.

FOOD VALUE: A tasty panfish and quite meaty for its size. The meat is white but flavorful. Best prepared by dressing and pan-frying whole.

GAME QUALITIES: Very aggressive, Sand Perch often hit baits and lures meant for much larger fish. However, their size and strength cannot match their attitude.

TACKLE AND BAITS: Sand Perch are often fished for deliberately, whether for supper or for bait (they are a staple bait among Gulf Tarpon fishermen, and also are excellent for grouper). Best tackle is a light spinning outfit. Small jigs, either plain or tipped with a piece of shrimp or cut bait, will produce the most, but any sort of bottom rig and natural bait will do the job.

FISHING SYSTEMS: Still Fishing; Drifting.

OTHER NAMES:
Coral Snapper
Squirrelfish
Bolo

RANGE: Both coasts of Florida, north to south. Apparently absent from the Bahamas.

HABITAT: Sand Perch are found from bays and shorelines to well offshore over a variety of bottoms. They seem to prefer rather open bottom with patches of grass or scattered rock, and they also like deep channels.

Although several members of the Porgy clan have plenty of admirers in Florida, the Sheepshead stands far above the others in overall popularity—due to its potentially large size, delicious fillets and widespread availability from boat or shore. In those respects, the Pinfish is at the other end of the scale, yet it's a pet of countless young anglers, for whom it often is a first catch, and is also revered by adult fishermen, if only for bait.

In between are several fish that actually wear "Porgy" as part of their common names. Various species, of which the ones included here are the most familiar, can be caught anywhere from the shoreline to the deep reefs, and though lacking the prestige of Snapper and Grouper, they aren't far behind them on the dinner table.

Note, however, that all the Porgies have a row of tiny bones along the centerline of the fillet, which must be cut out. The Scup—a Porgy well known to anglers transplanted from the mid and upper Atlantic states—is rare in Florida and is not included here.

8

The Porgies

Sheepshead
Pinfish
Spottail Pinfish
Silver Porgy
Sea Bream
Grass Porgy
Knobbed Porgy
Whitebone Porgy
Jolthead Porgy
Saucereye Porgy
Red Porgy

Sheepshead

Archosargus probatocephalus

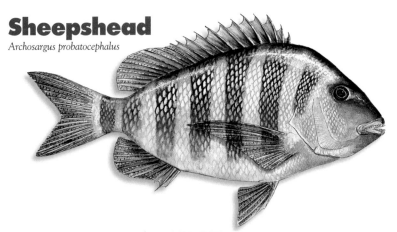

OTHER NAMES:
Convict Fish
Bait-stealer

RANGE: *All Florida salt waters.*

HABITAT: *Areas of rocky bottom, from far up coastal creeks and rivers, to well offshore. Loves dock and bridge pilings, artificial reefs and any other structure that wears barnacles and/or harbors crabs. Forages for crustaceans, at times, on shallow soft-bottom flats in the manner of Redfish or Bonefish.*

DESCRIPTION: Black vertical bands stand out against a dull white, gray or yellowish background. The mouth is full of massive, protruding teeth that give the fish its name, and distinguish it from the juvenile Black Drum (Chapter 1), the only fish with which it is likely to be confused. Spines of the dorsal and anal fins are heavy and sharp.

SIZE: Common from less than a pound to 4 pounds. Fairly plentiful at 5-7 pounds. Fish approaching 10 pounds, and occasionally surpassing 10, are taken each year in North Florida, especially from offshore wrecks and navigation markers in late winter and spring. World record 21 pounds, 4 ounces; Florida record 15 pounds, 2 ounces.

FOOD VALUE: One of the best, thanks in great part to its shellfish diet.

GAME QUALITIES: Not an aggressive strike; very tough on light tackle. Pulls hard and uses flat shape to advantage.

TACKLE AND BAITS: Light spinning and baitcasting tackle are tops for sport, but rodtip should not be too soft, as the tough and toothy mouth makes it hard to set a hook. Best baits are fiddlers or other small crabs; cut pieces of blue crab; live or fresh-dead shrimp (threaded on the hook); pieces of oysters and clams. Sheepshead will readily hit slow-moving jigs tipped with these baits and, occasionally, will take the bare jig.

FISHING SYSTEMS: Still Fishing.

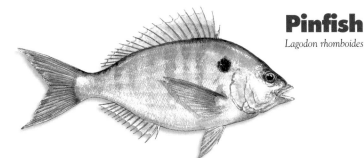

Pinfish
Lagodon rhomboides

DESCRIPTION: Silvery with many narrow longitudinal yellow lines and, sometimes, dim vertical bars. Dark patch just behind gill cover. Spines of dorsal and anal fin are sharp, hence the name.

SIZE: Most run 3-6 inches, but may range as high as a pound or more. World record 3 pounds, 5 ounces.

FOOD VALUE: Only the largest are really suitable for the table; small ones have excessive and tiny bones.

GAME QUALITIES: An aggressive striker and zippy fighter, much like a small Jack.

TACKLE AND BAITS: Bits of cut shrimp, fish, or bacon, fished on tiny hooks with canepoles or spinning outfits, will catch the most.

FISHING SYSTEMS: Drifting; Still Fishing.

OTHER NAMES:
Spanish Porgy
Shiner
Sargo
Chopo Sina

RANGE: All Florida coasts.

HABITAT: Small pinfish swarm over inshore grass flats in warm or temperate weather, retreating to deeper water with dropping temperatures. They also can be found around other cover, such as rocks and bars.

Spottail Pinfish
Diplodus holbrooki

DESCRIPTION: Somewhat rounder in shape than the Pinfish. Color is brownish above, silvery below. The name comes from a black patch on caudal peduncle.

SIZE: Averages 6-8 inches; grows to a pound or so.

FOOD VALUE: Often large enough to make a decent panfish—but watch those bones!

GAME QUALITIES: A good fighter for its size.

TACKLE AND BAITS: Light spinning outfits with cut shrimp, squid or fish.

FISHING SYSTEMS: Still Fishing; Drifting.

OTHER NAMES:
Spot Porgy
San Pedra

RANGE: All Florida coasts.

HABITAT: Seems to roam farther offshore than the Pinfish, although the two often mix around shorelines.

Silver Porgy
Diplodus argenteus

RANGE: *More common in the Bahamas, but also found in Florida, especially Southeast Florida.*

HABITAT: *Likes reefs or rocks in clear, shallow water. Many are taken from Bahamas shorelines.*

DESCRIPTION: Confused with the Spottail Pinfish because both have a black spot on the caudal peduncle. However, the Silver Porgy's spot is both lighter and proportionately smaller. This fish is also lighter in color and has thin yellowish stripes and, often, dark vertical bars.

SIZE: Averages 6-8 inches; rarely exceeds a pound.

FOOD VALUE: Good but bony.

GAME QUALITIES: Strong and fast for its size.

TACKLE AND BAITS: Ultralight or light spinning tackle, baited with bits of cut fish or shellfish.

FISHING SYSTEMS: Still Fishing; Drifting.

Sea Bream
Archosargus rhomboidalis

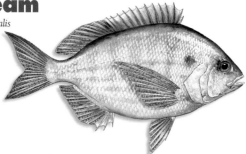

OTHER NAMES:
Golden Pinfish
Golden Shiner
Chopa Amarilla
Salema

RANGE: *All Florida coasts and the Bahamas.*

HABITAT: *Likes rockier bottom than the Pinfish. Common around jetties, and around rocky areas of surf and shorelines.*

DESCRIPTION: Silvery color with numerous yellow stripes that give it a golden sheen. Deeper bodied than the Pinfish, and usually larger.

SIZE: Average is 8-12 inches; maximum about 14 inches.

FOOD VALUE: Good but bony.

GAME QUALITIES: A cooperative biter and good tussler for its size.

TACKLE AND BAITS: Light spinning and baitcasting outfits. Live or dead shrimp and cut fish or squid.

FISHING SYSTEMS: Drifting; Still Fishing.

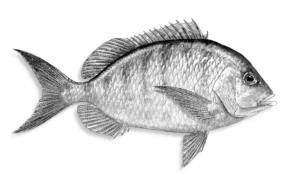

Grass Porgy

Calamus arctifrons

DESCRIPTION: Upper body greenish; silvery sides with dark blotches over sides and tail, often resembling a camouflage pattern. Dark vertical bar through eye.

SIZE: Averages around 1 pound; seldom grows larger.

FOOD VALUE: Good.

GAME QUALITIES: Strong for its size.

TACKLE AND BAITS: Light spinning and baitcasting tackle, with live or dead shrimp and various cut baits. Usually taken when fishing for Snapper or Seatrout.

FISHING SYSTEMS: Still Fishing; Drifting.

OTHER NAMES:
Grass Bream
Shad Porgy

RANGE: Both coasts of Florida.

HABITAT: Grass beds in up to 20 feet or so of water.

Knobbed Porgy

Calamus nodosus

DESCRIPTION: Color is a silvery with reddish tint. Head is steeply sloped and front edge is purple.

SIZE: Common up to 4 pounds; occasionally larger. World record 5 pounds 12 ounces.

FOOD VALUE: Excellent.

GAME QUALITIES: A strong if unspectacular fighter.

TACKLE AND BAITS: Most are caught deep by anglers seeking Grouper and Snapper; thus, the usual gear is fairly heavy ocean tackle. Stout baitcasting or spinning outfits are better suited to the task, however. Cut pieces of fish or squid are preferred baits.

FISHING SYSTEMS: Still Fishing; Drifting.

OTHER NAMES:
Key West Porgy

RANGE: All Florida coasts and the Bahamas.

HABITAT: Usually caught over coral reefs or patchy bottom in 70 feet of water or more.

Whitebone Porgy

Calamus leucosteus

OTHER NAMES:
White Porgy
Silver Porgy
Silver Snapper

RANGE: *All Florida coasts and the Bahamas.*

HABITAT: *Usually in fairly deep water, 15-100 feet, over rocks, reefs or patchy bottom.*

DESCRIPTION: Color is a silvery white, sometimes with dark blotches or patterns. Blue lines on head.

SIZE: Common up to 4 pounds; occasionally larger.

FOOD VALUE: Very good; bones can be filleted out.

GAME QUALITIES: Close to Snappers of similar size.

TACKLE AND BAITS: As with other reef Porgies, most are caught by anglers seeking Grouper and Snapper with fairly heavy ocean tackle. Stout baitcasting or spinning outfits are better suited to the task, however. Cut pieces of fish or squid are preferred baits.

FISHING SYSTEMS: Still Fishing; Drifting.

Jolthead Porgy

Calamus bajonado

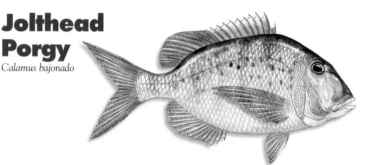

OTHER NAMES:
Bajonado

RANGE: *All Florida coasts and the Bahamas.*

HABITAT: *Found over inshore grass flats as well as on offshore reefs and patches.*

DESCRIPTION: Head is more sharply sloped than that of other Porgies. Color is silvery with blue highlights. Brownish pattern may be evident in fish caught over dark bottom, but most are light.

SIZE: One of the largest Porgies, it averages a couple of pounds and sometimes more. World record 23 pounds, 4 ounces.

FOOD VALUE: Very good, if large enough to fillet.

GAME QUALITIES: Unspectacular but strong.

TACKLE AND BAITS: Light spinning and baitcasting outfits, with any sort of cut fish, shrimp or squid.

FISHING SYSTEMS: Still Fishing; Drifting.

Saucereye Porgy
Calamus calamus

DESCRIPTION: The Saucereye's name is derived from a blue line below the eye that causes the eye to appear larger. Color usually is silvery, with the blue streaks that are common to several of the Porgies.

SIZE: Common at 2-3 pounds; reaches perhaps 7 or 8.

FOOD VALUE: Very good.

GAME QUALITIES: A strong puller.

TACKLE AND BAITS: Most are caught deep by anglers seeking Grouper and Snapper with heavy tackle. Stout baitcasting or spinning outfits are better suited, however. Cut fish or squid.

FISHING SYSTEMS: Still Fishing; Drifting.

OTHER NAMES:
Big-eye Porgy
Pez De Pluma

RANGE: *Both Florida coasts and the Bahamas.*

HABITAT: *Usually in fairly deep water, up to 100 feet.*

Red Porgy
Pagrus pagrus

DESCRIPTION: Light, reddish silver overall, with pinkish tail.

SIZE: Averages 2-10 pounds; may reach 20 or more. World record 17 pounds.

FOOD VALUE: Excellent.

GAME QUALITIES: Not much, considering gear used.

TACKLE AND BAITS: Heavy bottom rigs, preferably with electric reels. Cut baits.

FISHING SYSTEMS: Drifting.

OTHER NAMES:
Guerito

RANGE: *Offshore depths of Florida and the Bahamas.*

HABITAT: *Dropoffs in at least 200 feet; also far deeper.*

Grunts are a primarily tropical family of fishes, various types of which are familiar to skindivers who explore coral reefs. Several of the many species, however, enjoy a much wider habitat, ranging well into temperate waters and so becoming available to North Floridians as well as to those who fish South Florida and the Bahamas. Although not considered great sport fish, Grunts are fun to catch and make fine table fare, ranking among the favorites of many old-timers and often providing a good fish dinner when Snapper and Grouper are uncooperative. Of numerous species that inhabit our waters, the following are the ones that are large enough to be of any interest to sport fishermen.

The Grunts

Pigfish

White Grunt

Margate

Bluestriped Grunt

French Grunt

Tomtate

Black Margate

Porkfish

Pigfish

Orthopristis chrysoptera

OTHER NAMES:

Grunt

Orange Grunt

Piggy

RANGE: *All Florida coasts and the Bahamas.*

HABITAT: *Unlike most Grunts, the Pigfish doesn't mind murky water or soft bottom, and makes itself at home in a variety of shallow-water habitats throughout the state. Although most are taken over grassy flats, they are also plentiful around bars and along channel edges.*

DESCRIPTION: Light brown or gray, with numerous small orange and blue markings and a small mouth.

SIZE: Common between 3 and 6 inches; may reach 10 or 12 inches.

FOOD VALUE: Larger ones make tasty panfish.

GAME QUALITIES: Pretty good puller, if hooked on light gear.

TACKLE AND BAITS: Small Pigfish are preferred live baits for Seatrout and other species—the thought being that their grunting attracts the predators from a goodly distance away. If you're seeking Pigfish for bait, use canepole or light spinning gear with small hooks and bits of cut bait or shrimp. Most Pigfish are caught, however, on tackle used for Seatrout on the grass flats. They are also popular potluck catches from docks and bridges, especially on the Gulf Coast. They will take shrimp, of course, and just about any size strip bait. They may hit jigs and small plugs.

FISHING SYSTEMS: Drifting; Still Fishing.

White Grunt

Haemulon plumieri

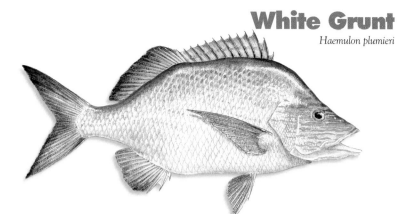

DESCRIPTION: Usually from light gray, almost white, to dark gray. Many small blue and yellow lines on head.

SIZE: Averages 8-10 inches; not too uncommon at 12 inches or slightly larger, especially in deeper waters of the Gulf. World record 6 pounds, 8 ounces.

FOOD VALUE: Very good, especially as part of the historic Florida dish, "Grits and Grunts." Usually served whole as panfish, but many Grunts are large enough to provide small fillets.

GAME QUALITIES: Strong if hooked on light tackle.

TACKLE AND BAITS: Spinning and plug casting outfits and light saltwater gear. Grunt fishermen usually choose cut baits, but the White Grunt also bites willingly on small jigs.

FISHING SYSTEMS: Still Fishing; Drifting.

OTHER NAMES:

Gray Grunt
Key West Grunt
Ronco Arara

RANGE: All Florida coasts and the Bahamas.

HABITAT: Sticks to coral reef bottom or rocky bottom, from near shore in many areas out to at least 100 feet deep. Fishermen consider good White Grunt bottom to be potentially good Grouper bottom as well.

Margate

Haemulon album

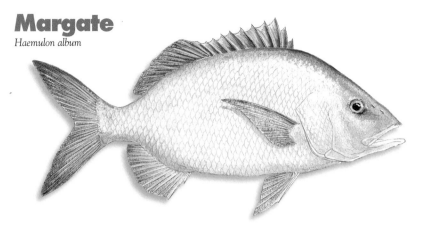

OTHER NAMES:
White Margate
Margate Grunt
Ronco Blanco

RANGE: *Rather plentiful in the Bahamas; occurs in Florida but is seen less often.*

HABITAT: *Off Florida, deeper reef waters—50-150 feet— turn up most Margates, but they roam into the shallows in many areas of the Bahamas.*

DESCRIPTION: Similar in shape to the White Grunt but color is solid white or pearly, with darker fins. The **Sailors Choice, Haemulon parra,** is a similar though smaller Grunt, distinguished by scaled pectoral fins. Note, however, that in Florida, the name Sailors Choice is more widely used for the Pinfish (see page 97).

SIZE: This is the largest of the Grunts, frequently running to 4 or 5 pounds, and reaching at least 12 pounds. World record 15 pounds, 12 ounces; Florida record 11 pounds, 4 ounces.

FOOD VALUE: Good. May have a strong odor or taste, which can be eliminated by freezing for a few days or by soaking in lightly salted water.

GAME QUALITIES: Very good. Fights much like a Snapper of equivalent size.

TACKLE AND BAITS: Difficult to target, most are caught on cut baits by bottom fishermen using fairly heavy ocean tackle, but some fall to deep jiggers using stout spinning and plug outfits. They will hit heavy jigs, especially if tipped with a plastic worm.

FISHING SYSTEMS: Still Fishing; Drifting.

Bluestriped Grunt

Haemulon sciurus

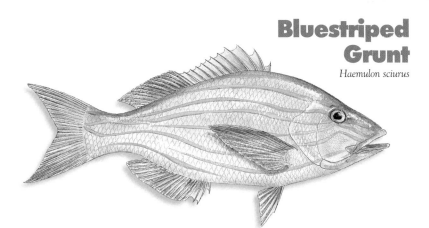

DESCRIPTION: Yellow body marked by numerous longitudinal blue stripes. Inside of mouth is red. Dark tail and dorsal fin.

SIZE: Averages 8-10 inches; sometimes exceeds 12.

FOOD VALUE: Very good.

GAME QUALITIES: A strong fighter on light gear.

TACKLE AND BAITS: Light spinning and baitcasting outfits. Live or dead shrimp and cut bait. Also hits small lures.

FISHING SYSTEMS: Still Fishing; Drifting.

OTHER NAMES:
Blue Grunt
Yellow Grunt
Ronco Amarillo

RANGE: *South Florida and the Bahamas.*

HABITAT: *Coral reefs; inshore patches and channels.*

French Grunt

Haemulon flavolineatum

OTHER NAMES:

Yellow Grunt
Corocoro
Ronco Contenado

RANGE: South Florida and the Bahamas.

HABITAT: Coral reefs; inshore patches and channels.

DESCRIPTION: Gray or white with numerous yellow stripes. Inside of mouth is red.

SIZE: Averages 6-8 inches; may rarely reach 12 inches.

FOOD VALUE: Very good.

GAME QUALITIES: Fun on very light gear.

TACKLE AND BAITS: Light spinning and baitcasting tackle; shrimp and cut baits.

FISHING SYSTEMS: Still Fishing; Drifting.

Tomtate

Haemulon aurolineatum

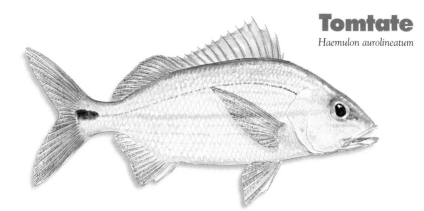

DESCRIPTION: White or silvery with a prominent brown or yellow stripe running from gill to tail. Thinner stripes may also be present.

SIZE: Usually about 6 inches; seldom larger.

FOOD VALUE: Small, but a good panfish.

GAME QUALITIES: Not big enough to do much.

TACKLE AND BAITS: Lightest spinning tackle; pieces of shrimp and cut fish or squid.

FISHING SYSTEMS: Still Fishing.

OTHER NAMES:

Brown Grunt
Jeniguano
Cuji

RANGE: Most of Florida and the Bahamas.

HABITAT: Inshore patches and offshore reefs of South Florida and the Bahamas; mostly offshore farther north.

Black Margate

Anisotremus surinamensis

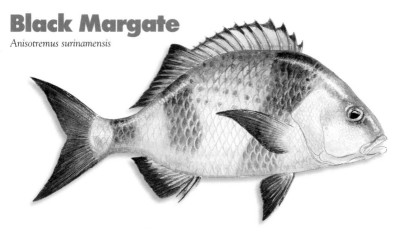

OTHER NAMES:
Black Bream
Surf Bream
Pompon

RANGE: Both coasts of Florida, but more common on Atlantic side. Also in the Bahamas.

HABITAT: Ranges widely, from near shore to outer reefs. Many are caught from surf in areas of groins or other rocky bottom.

DESCRIPTION: Although a member of the Grunt family, the Black Margate superficially appears more closely allied to the Croakers or Drums. The body is deep, the dorsal spines heavy and the lips thick. Sides are dingy white, with a prominent black band or saddle around the body. The fins are dark gray or black.

SIZE: Another large Grunt, this one often reaches 3 or 4 pounds and may top 10. World and Florida records 12 pounds, 12 ounces.

FOOD VALUE: Good.

GAME QUALITIES: Exhibits good strength and stamina on light gear.

TACKLE AND BAITS: Spinning, baitcasting and surf tackle. Light classes of ocean tackle. Shrimp and clams are excellent baits, but cut fish works well too. Rarely takes artificials.

FISHING SYSTEMS: Still Fishing; Drifting.

Porkfish

Anisotremus virginicus

DESCRIPTION: Deep body shape is similar to that of the Black Margate. Thick lips. One of the brightest of the Grunts. Gold or silvery sheen with two vertical black bars, one through the head and another running from the dorsal to the pectoral fin. Longitudinal bronze and blue stripes. World record 2 pounds, 3 ounces.

SIZE: Averages 8-10 inches; reaches 14 inches or more.

FOOD VALUE: Good.

GAME QUALITIES: Tough battler for its size.

TACKLE AND BAITS: Light spinning and baitcasting outfits; shrimp and cut baits.

FISHING SYSTEMS: Still Fishing.

OTHER NAMES:

Harlequin Grunt

Sisi

Catalineta

RANGE: South Florida and the Bahamas.

HABITAT: Coral reefs and inshore patches.

Reef fishermen mostly take aim at Snappers and Groupers. Failing those, they take solace in Grunts and Porgies. But there are other fish down there that they often have to take, whether they like it or not! At least a few, including the Hogfish and Triggerfish, are widely prized as table fare.

The Triggerfishes get their name because—as you may have guessed—they are fitted with a "trigger." When the forward dorsal spine stands erect, no amount of pressure the angler can exert will force it down, yet a slight push on the shorter second spine—the trigger—will fold it instantly.

Wrasses and Parrotfishes belong to separate but related families that share many characteristics, prominent among them being protruding teeth and large, heavy scales. However, the teeth of the Parrotfishes—which give them their common name—are much more impressive than those of the Wrasses. Only one fish from either group is of significant interest to anglers, that being the Hogfish—a large and spectacular-looking Wrasse that is ranked among the best of table fishes.

The Angelfishes are beauties of the coral reefs that are sometimes caught on hook and line. The Spadefish is not really an Angelfish but is grouped with them here because of similar appearance.

A few reef fish are downright menacing, such as the various types of Scorpionfishes and Morays, of which only the species most commonly caught by anglers are included here.

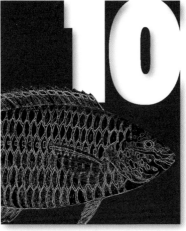

Miscellaneous Reef Fish

Hogfish
Lachnolaimus maximus

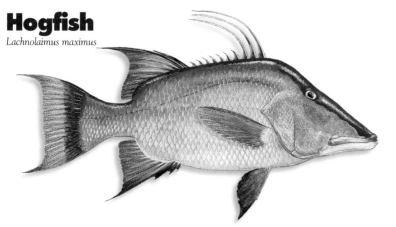

OTHER NAMES:
Hog Snapper
Hog Wrasse
Captain
Perro Perro
Pargo Gallo

RANGE: *Offshore over deep structure in most of Florida; also on inshore patches in South Florida and the Bahamas.*

HABITAT: *Coral reefs and rocky areas.*

DESCRIPTION: Deep body; long tapering mouth with protruding teeth. Color varies but is usually a soft red. Very large specimens have a diagonal purple band running from dorsal fin to snout, and the first three rays of the dorsal fin are elongated into streamers. Tail and anal fin also sport more modest streamers.

SIZE: Average catch runs 1-4 pounds; maximum size is over 20 pounds. Fish exceeding about 6 pounds are now unusual in Florida, although still fairly plentiful in some areas of the Bahamas and the Caribbean. World record 21 pounds, 9 ounces; Florida record 19 pounds, 8 ounces.

FOOD VALUE: Outstanding. With its very fine, white flesh, the Hog Snapper is considered by many anglers, and spearfishermen, as the prize of all reef species for the table.

GAME QUALITIES: They pull fairly well when first hooked, but don't have much stamina, compared to the true Snappers. Most fishermen care less about the battle than the fillets.

TACKLE AND BAITS: Spinning, baitcasting and light ocean tackle. Although Hog Snapper occasionally take pieces of cut fish, crustacean baits are almost a must. Best are pieces of lobster and crab, or live shrimp. Other parts of shellfish, such as shrimp heads and lobster legs, make excellent chum.

FISHING SYSTEMS: Still Fishing.

Gray Triggerfish

Balistes capriscus

DESCRIPTION: Uniform dark gray in color, sometimes with darker blotches on the sides, especially in smaller fish.

SIZE: Averages 1-3 pounds; may rarely top 10 pounds. World record 13 pounds, 9 ounces. Florida record 12 pounds, 7 ounces.

FOOD VALUE: Excellent. Many consider Triggerfish fillets to be tastier fare than those from the Yellowtail and small Snapper that are often caught with them in mixed bags. They are, however, more difficult to clean because of their tough skins.

GAME QUALITIES: The small mouth of the Triggerfish makes them difficult to hook, but once they are on a line they put up an outstanding fight against light tackle.

TACKLE AND BAITS: Spinning, baitcasting and light ocean tackle. Small hooks are essential. They bite shrimp and any sort of cut bait and also nip voraciously at artificial lures, especially plastics, although seldom getting hooked on them.

FISHING SYSTEMS: Still Fishing; Drifting.

OTHER NAMES:

Common
    Triggerfish
Common Turbot
Cucuyo

RANGE: All Florida, the Bahamas and Caribbean.

HABITAT: Mostly found well off-shore in northern half of Florida, but inhabits both inshore areas—patches, holes, bridge and dock pilings—and offshore reefs of South Florida, the Bahamas and the Caribbean Islands.

Queen Triggerfish

Balistes vetula

RANGE: *Very common on Bahamas and Caribbean reefs. Fairly common on South Florida reefs and can be encountered offshore in most of Florida.*

HABITAT: *Coral reefs.*

DESCRIPTION: Variably marked but always garish. The overall color ranges from blue to greenish. The mouth is circled in bright blue and two or more blue lines run from snout to pectoral fin. Gold markings around eyes and, often, other lines and marks on rear of body. Blue band around caudal peduncle. Long trailing edges on dorsal and caudal fins.

SIZE: From a couple of pounds to more than 5 pounds and, rarely, to 10 or 12 pounds. World record 12 pounds.

FOOD VALUE: Excellent.

GAME QUALITIES: Tough battler on light tackle.

TACKLE AND BAITS: Spinning, baitcasting and light ocean tackle. Small hooks are essential. Will bite any sort of cut bait and also nip voraciously at artificial lures, especially plastics.

FISHING SYSTEMS: Still Fishing; Drifting.

Ocean Triggerfish
Canthidermis sufflamen

DESCRIPTION: Overall dark gray or black. Black blotch at base of pectoral fin.

SIZE: On average, the largest of the Triggers, commonly weighing 4-6 pounds; sometimes tops 10 pounds. World record 13 pounds, 8 ounces.

FOOD VALUE: Good but tends to be coarser than other Triggers.

GAME QUALITIES: A very strong and stubborn fighter.

TACKLE AND BAITS: Spinning, baitcasting and light ocean tackle. Small hooks and baits are essential. Will bite any sort of cut bait. Also takes jigs, and even flies.

FISHING SYSTEMS: Still Fishing; Drift Fishing.

OTHER NAMES:
Ocean Tally
Great Trigger
Turbot

RANGE: *All Florida, Bahamas, Caribbean.*

HABITAT: *Mostly encountered well offshore, but often ventures to reef areas, and sometimes to shallow flats in the Keys and islands.*

Puddingwife "Green Wrasse"
Halichoeres radiatus

DESCRIPTION: Color varies from light to brilliant green, with yellow and pinkish highlights and numerous blue lines.

SIZE: Usually around 1 pound; runs to at least 3.

FOOD VALUE: Not often eaten, but quite good.

GAME QUALITIES: Not much.

TACKLE AND BAITS: Spinning tackle with small hooks and bits of shrimp or cut fish.

FISHING SYSTEMS: Still Fishing.

OTHER NAMES:
Doncella

RANGE: *South Florida and the Bahamas; sometimes caught in temperate waters of Florida.*

HABITAT: *Coral reefs and rocks.*

Queen Parrotfish

Scarus vetula

OTHER NAMES:

Vieja

RANGE: *South Florida and the Bahamas.*

HABITAT: *Coral reefs.*

DESCRIPTION: Adult males are deep green with yellow highlights on their scales and fins. Black, wavy lines around mouth. Female is a dull brown with a yellowish stripe on side.

SIZE: Up to 2 feet or so.

FOOD VALUE: Not usually eaten.

GAME QUALITIES: Rarely hooked, but strong.

TACKLE AND BAITS: Occasionally takes a crustacean bait fished by reef fishermen.

FISHING SYSTEMS: Not targeted.

Blue Parrotfish

Scarus coeruleus

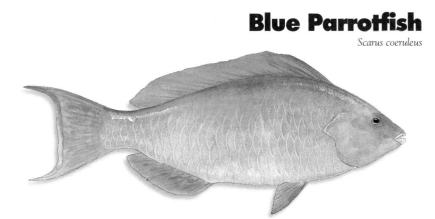

DESCRIPTION: Adult males deep blue all over; young and females lighter blue, with some yellow on head and dorsal fin.

SIZE: Up to 2 feet or so.

FOOD VALUE: Not usually eaten.

GAME QUALITIES: Rarely hooked, but strong.

TACKLE AND BAITS: Occasionally takes a crustacean bait fished by reef fishermen.

FISHING SYSTEMS: Not targeted.

OTHER NAMES:
Loro Azul

RANGE: *South Florida and the Bahamas.*

HABITAT: *Coral reefs.*

Rainbow Parrotfish

Scarus guacamaia

DESCRIPTION: On large males, head and shoulders are gold, as are the fins. Scales on rest of body are deep green or aqua, ringed in gold. Red streaks or spots around pectoral fins. Blue mouth. Females and small males are mostly green with small patches of gold on the head and fins.

SIZE: The largest of our Parrotfishes, it often exceeds three feet in length.

FOOD VALUE: Not usually eaten.

GAME QUALITIES: Rarely hooked, but strong.

TACKLE AND BAITS: Occasionally takes a crustacean bait fished by reef fishermen.

FISHING SYSTEMS: Not targeted.

Blue Angelfish

Holacanthus bermudensis

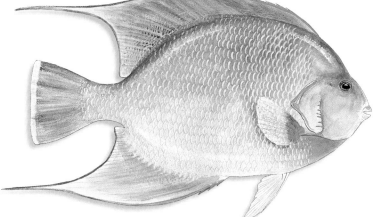

DESCRIPTION: Body is yellowish with blue highlights and blue-tipped dorsal and anal spines. Tail is yellow. Very similar to the Queen Angelfish, but lacks the blue spots on forehead and pectoral. May hybridize with the Queen Angel.

SIZE: Up to about 18 inches.

FOOD VALUE: Seldom eaten; said to be okay.

GAME QUALITIES: Rarely hooked.

TACKLE AND BAITS: Caught once in a while by reef fishermen on shrimp and cut baits, but feeds mostly on sponges and other tropical marine growth.

FISHING SYSTEMS: Still Fishing but not targeted.

RANGE: Mostly South Florida and Bahamas; some off both coasts of North Florida.

HABITAT: Prefers coral reefs and areas with sponges.

French Angelfish

Pomacanthus paru

OTHER NAMES:

Black Angelfish
Cachama Negra
Chirivita

RANGE: *Mostly South Florida, Bahamas and Caribbean, but some off both coasts of North Florida.*

HABITAT: *Prefers coral reefs and areas with sponges.*

DESCRIPTION: Body is black with yellow-edged scales. Yellow edge on dorsal fin and gill cover. Yellow spot at base of pectoral fin.

SIZE: Up to about 15 inches.

FOOD VALUE: Seldom eaten; said to be okay.

GAME QUALITIES: Seldom hooked; spirited fighter on light gear.

TACKLE AND BAITS: Caught once in a while by reef fishermen, but feeds mostly on sponges and other marine growth.

FISHING SYSTEMS: Still Fishing but not targeted.

Queen Angelfish

Holacanthus ciliaris

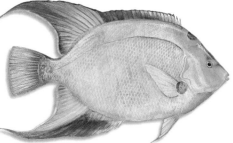

OTHER NAMES:

Isabellita
Cachama De
Piedra

RANGE: *Mostly South Florida, the Bahamas and Caribbean; some off both coasts of North Florida.*

HABITAT: *Prefers coral reefs and areas with plenty of sponges.*

DESCRIPTION: Mostly yellow but bright blue markings on the head, and blue edges on dorsal and anal fins. Black spot, ringed with blue, on forehead. Dark blue spot at base of pectoral.

SIZE: Most run 12-18 inches.

FOOD VALUE: Seldom eaten; said to be okay.

GAME QUALITIES: Rarely hooked.

TACKLE AND BAITS: Caught once in a while by reef fishermen on shrimp and cut baits, but feeds mostly on sponges and other tropical marine growth.

FISHING SYSTEMS: Still Fishing but not targeted.

Atlantic Spadefish

Chaetodipterus faber

DESCRIPTION: Deep, rounded body. First rays of posterior, dorsal and anal fin are long and pointed. Color: black vertical bands on a grayish white background. Bands may be vague or almost missing in large specimens.

SIZE: Averages 2-3 pounds; occasionally tops 10. World record 14 pounds.

FOOD VALUE: Good.

GAME QUALITIES: Difficult to hook, but a strong, Jack-like fighter.

TACKLE AND BAITS: Spinning and plug casting tackle. Though Spadefish are taken on shrimp, and sometimes on cut fish, they are usually picky biters. Their natural diet is heavy on jellyfish.

FISHING SYSTEMS: Still Fishing.

OTHER NAMES:
Striped Angelfish
Chrivita Chiva

RANGE: All Florida coasts, the Bahamas and Caribbean.

HABITAT: Likes a variety of structure, from mangroves to corals. Common around navigation markers and pilings in deep channels and sometimes well offshore.

Bermuda Chub

Kyphosus sectatrix

OTHER NAMES:

Sea Chub
Butter Bream
Chopa

RANGE: South Florida, the Bahamas and the Caribbean. Infrequently seen in other Florida areas.

HABITAT: Clear reefs and grass patches from near shore to deep reefs. Also encountered sometimes in the open seas, around sargassum weeds.

DESCRIPTION: The Bermuda Chub shown here, and the **Yellow Chub**, *Kyphosus incisor*, are so nearly identical in appearance and habits that it would be a rare angler who could tell them apart—or wish to. Both are oval-shaped with forked tails. Color of both is gray or blue with many narrow, full-length yellow stripes on the sides. These stripes are somewhat more obvious and lustrous in the Yellow Chub than in the Bermuda.

SIZE: Averages 2-3 pounds; often exceeds 5 pounds and can reach 10 or more. World records: Bermuda Chub 13 pounds, 4 ounces; Yellow Chub 8 pounds, 8 ounces.

FOOD VALUE: Edible but mushy and strong-flavored.

GAME QUALITIES: A very strong fighter.

TACKLE AND BAITS: Spinning, baitcasting and light ocean outfits provide the best sport. Chubs are vegetarians, but take cut baits at times. If they are hanging around and you wish to target them, the best baits are bread balls or scraps of lettuce and cabbage.

FISHING SYSTEMS: Still Fishing; Drift Fishing.

Squirrelfish

Holocentrus adscensionis

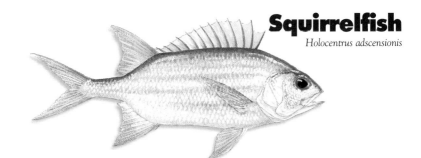

DESCRIPTION: A colorful little fish, mostly light red or pink with streaks of white or silver. Fins are spiny and prominent; tail deeply forked. Eye large. Several other species occur in the tropics.

SIZE: Less than a foot.

FOOD VALUE: Edible but hardly worth the effort. Care must be taken in handling because of razor-sharp gill covers and sharp spines on dorsal and anal fins.

GAME QUALITIES: Virtually none. Mainly of interest only as another of the many small species that a reef fisherman sometimes brings up.

TACKLE AND BAITS: Would offer any sport at all only on the lightest of spinning tackle. Hits many cut baits.

OTHER NAMES:
Soldierfish
Candil

RANGE: *South Florida, the Bahamas and the Caribbean.*

HABITAT: *Coral reefs; also inshore patches.*

Bigeye "Toro"

Priacanthus arenatus

DESCRIPTION: Compressed body of solid brick red. Large eye. Very large mouth.

SIZE: Less than a foot long. World record 6 pounds, 4 ounces.

FOOD VALUE: Pretty good; not much meat.

GAME QUALITIES: Minor.

TACKLE AND BAITS: All sorts of bottom-fishing tackle; small cut baits.

FISHING SYSTEMS: Still Fishing.

OTHER NAMES:
Comico

RANGE: *South Florida, the Bahamas and the Caribbean.*

HABITAT: *Coral reefs and rocky areas, usually from 30 feet or so to very deep ledges.*

Spotted Scorpionfish

Scorpaena plumieri

OTHER NAMES:

Lionfish
Rascacio

RANGE: *One or more species may be encountered nearly any-where in Florida waters, but most are tropical fish inhabiting South Florida, the Bahamas and the Caribbean.*

HABITAT: *Coral reefs and patches; rocky areas.*

DESCRIPTION: Several species occur in Florida and the Tropics, of which the one most familiar to anglers is the rather large Spotted Scorpionfish, shown here. Scorpions have many spikes dotted over the head and gill covers, but their main defensive weapons are the dorsal spines, which carry venom that can be painful and debilitating to a careless angler, but not fatal. Color is usually a mottled red or brown. Pectoral fins large and fanlike.

SIZE: Up to a foot; usually less. World record 3 pounds, 7 ounces.

FOOD VALUE: Fishermen wisely avoid handling them, but if large enough to bother with, they make very good eating.

GAME QUALITIES: None.

TACKLE AND BAITS: Reef-fishing outfits with cut baits.

FISHING SYSTEMS: Still Fishing.

Green Moray

Gymnothorax funebris

DESCRIPTION: Largest of the Morays. Green overall.

SIZE: Common at 4-5 feet; exceeds 7 feet. World record 33 pounds, 8 ounces.

FOOD VALUE: Unappetizing at best, and also implicated in Ciguatera poisoning (see Introduction).

GAME QUALITIES: Tough to pull out of its hole, but its biggest fight comes after landing, when it likes to tie itself—and the fishing line—into knots.

TACKLE AND BAITS: Never targeted, it's usually caught on bottom-fishing tackle of various sorts.

FISHING SYSTEMS: Still Fishing.

OTHER NAMES:
Green Eel
Morena Verde

RANGE: *All Florida coasts, but most common in South Florida, the Bahamas and the Caribbean.*

HABITAT: *At home wherever there are holes or crevices—typically, coral reefs, but also jetties, pilings and nearshore rubble.*

Spotted Moray

Gymnothorax moringa

DESCRIPTION: White or yellowish with many dark brown spots that vary in size.

SIZE: Common at 1-2 feet; seldom longer than 3 feet. World record 5 pounds, 8 ounces.

FOOD VALUE: None. See Green Moray.

GAME QUALITIES: None. See Green Moray.

TACKLE AND BAITS: The catch usually comes as a surprise while bottom-fishing with cut bait.

FISHING SYSTEMS: Still Fishing.

OTHER NAMES:
Morena Pintada

RANGE: *South Florida, the Bahamas and the Caribbean.*

HABITAT: *Seems to prefer clear water, but found from shoreline to deep coral reefs.*

Sand Tilefish

Malacanthus plumieri

OTHER NAMES:

Sand Eel

Blanquillo

RANGE: *Both Florida coasts, but more common in Atlantic. Also Bahamas.*

HABITAT: *Sandy bottom, often around edges of coral reefs, mostly from 40 to 150 feet of water.*

DESCRIPTION: A slender, smooth-skinned fish with crescent tail. Color is cream or tan, sometimes with blue highlights. Anal fin extends nearly the length of the underside between ventral fin and tail.

SIZE: Usually 2 pounds or less. World record 4 pounds, 4 ounces.

FOOD VALUE: Pretty good, but seldom eaten; considered a throwback by most fishermen.

GAME QUALITIES: Poor.

TACKLE AND BAITS: Nobody fishes for Sand Eels. Most are unwelcome catches of reef fishermen seeking Snapper and Grouper. If you catch a Sand Eel it should be taken as sign of poor (meaning sandy) bottom. Hits any kind of cut bait.

FISHING SYSTEMS: Drifting; Still Fishing.

Tilefish

Lopholatilus chamaeleonticeps

DESCRIPTION: Color is gray or bluish, with numerous yellow dots. Head is blunt. A fleshy protuberance forward of the dorsal fin, and entirely separate from it, is a sure identifier. A similar species, the **Goldface Tilefish, *Caulolatilus Chrysops,*** has no fleshy protuberance but has a gold band on its head from eye to mouth.

SIZE: Common at 5-10 pounds; sometimes exceeds 20.

FOOD VALUE: Good. During periods of abundance, the Tilefish is popular commercially, but rated as less desirable for the table than deepwater Snappers and Groupers.

GAME QUALITIES: Largely irrelevant because Tilefish are nearly always caught on very heavy tackle or commercial electric rigs.

TACKLE AND BAITS: Charterboat anglers sometimes fish for Tilefish with wire lines and powered reels. It's exhausting work to crank them up with heavy manual tackle. Chunks of cut fish make good bait.

FISHING SYSTEMS: Drifting.

OTHER NAMES:
Blue Tilefish
Common Tilefish

RANGE: *All Florida coasts, but this fish varies greatly in abundance, evidently because of cycles that may be tied to vagaries of ocean currents. Tilefish also occur off the Bahamas, but are seldom caught there, due to lack of fishing effort.*

HABITAT: *Likes soft bottom with scattered rocks or growth. Most Florida fish are taken from depths of 400 feet or more.*

From a sportfishing standpoint, Billfishes are the true kings of the open sea. They are not only among the fastest of all fishes, but also the most spectacular in the battles they wage against the latest in sophisticated boats and tackle, handled by the most experienced of anglers and crews. Moreover, two of our Billfishes—Blue Marlin and Swordfish—also rank among the largest fish in the sea, being surpassed only by certain Sharks and matched only by the Giant Bluefin Tuna. White Marlin, Sailfish and Spearfish are lightweights by comparison, but are even more acrobatic than their larger cousins and are equally esteemed—if matched to suitable tackle. Sailfish from the Atlantic and Pacific oceans are actually the same species, though sails in the Pacific grow a good bit larger. One Billfish covered here—the Hatchet Marlin—is not yet accepted by science as a separate species, although several catches have been authenticated from the Gulf of Mexico and South Atlantic. Opinion is divided as to whether the Hatchet Marlin is a new type or simply a variation of the White Marlin.

The Billfishes

Swordfish

Blue Marlin

White Marlin

Hatchet Marlin

Longbill Spearfish

Sailfish

Swordfish

Xiphias gladius

OTHER NAMES:

Broadbill
Swordfish
Pez Espada

RANGE: *All deep ocean waters of Florida, the Bahamas and the Caribbean.*

HABITAT: *The deep sea.*

DESCRIPTION: A chunky and powerfully built fish with a high, crescent-shaped dorsal fin and broadly forked tail. The pectoral fins are also large and lunate. The distinguishing feature, however, is the huge bill or sword—much longer and wider than the bills of Marlins and Sailfish. The eye is also very large. Color is mostly dark brown to purple, with whitish undersides.

SIZE: Historically, from 100 to more than 1,000 pounds; however, relentless and virtually unregulated commercial longline fishing has lowered the average to well under 50 pounds. World record 1,182 pounds; Florida record 612 pounds, 4 ounces.

FOOD VALUE: Among the very best, which is helping skid the species toward oblivion.

GAME QUALITIES: Not as wild or acrobatic as the Blue Marlin, but an equally powerful and rugged fighter that can get off some spectacular jumps on occasion.

TACKLE AND BAITS: Although big fish are now rare, Swordfish are hooked so seldom that anyone who fishes for them is advised to use at least 50-pound line, matched to good ocean tackle. The best Swordfish bait always has been a large, rigged natural squid, but rigged baitfishes can work. During the 1970s, many Swordfish topping 400 pounds were caught by sportsmen, who fished by choice on calm nights, mostly during the summer, but also during good weather in fall and winter, and generally deployed two or more baits at different depths. The majority of strikes came at 100 feet or deeper.

FISHING SYSTEMS: Drifting.

Blue Marlin

Makaira nigricans

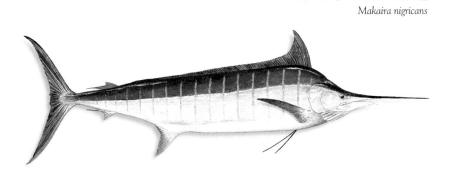

DESCRIPTION: Coloration varies a great deal. Most common phase is dark blue, almost black on the dorsal surface, shading to whitish. Usually, several vertical stripes are noticeable. Early in the 20th century, these variations led anglers to believe several species were involved. Science eventually determined that the Black and Striped Marlins are strictly Pacific species and that a Silver Marlin is non-existent. The Blue, however, is found in both hemispheres. The feature that distinguishes the Blue from others is the pointed dorsal fin that curves sharply downward. The anal fin and pectoral fins also are pointed.

SIZE: From about 150 pounds to 500; not rare over 500. World record 1,402 pounds; Florida record 1046 pounds.

FOOD VALUE: Good, but normally released by sportsmen; protected from sale in North Atlantic.

GAME QUALITIES: Best of all for speed, power and jumping ability.

TACKLE AND BAITS: While many Blues have been caught on lighter outfits, the standard is a good, balanced ocean trolling outfit in the 50-pound or even 80-pound line class. Marlin baits fall into three categories: 1. Artificial trolling lures; 2. Live, fairly large baitfish, such as school Dolphin or Bonito; and 3. Rigged natural baits, such as Mullet, Mackerel, Bonito, Barracuda, extra-large Ballyhoo ("Horse Ballyhoo"). Lures are used most often, because they allow more ocean to be covered. In somewhat limited areas, such as along weedlines or around seamounts and other well-established grounds, live bait is usually preferred.

FISHING SYSTEMS: Trolling; sometimes Drifting.

OTHER NAMES:
Aguja Azul

RANGE: *All deep blue offshore waters of Florida, the Bahamas and the Caribbean.*

HABITAT: *A free-roamer that is best fished where bait is most plentiful—along weedlines; around schools of small tuna and other pelagic baitfishes; in areas where seamounts or other sub-surface structure creates upwellings and current; sharp bottom contours; temperature changes.*

White Marlin

Tetrapturus albidus

OTHER NAMES:

Spikefish

Aguja Blanco

RANGE: *Blue ocean water off all Florida coasts and throughout the Bahamas and the Caribbean.*

HABITAT: *Like the Blue Marlin, a roamer of the open sea, and sought by anglers wherever feeding conditions or temperatures are most favorable.*

DESCRIPTION: Similar in color to the Blue Marlin but proportionately lighter in body; Whites can be distinguished from small Blues by the rounded tips of dorsal, anal and pectoral fins.

SIZE: Averages 40-70 pounds; 100-pounders not too uncommon; maximum less than 200. World record 181 pounds, 14 ounces; Florida record 161 pounds.

FOOD VALUE: Good but commercially protected and seldom eaten by sportsmen.

GAME QUALITIES: Probably the most aerial-minded of our Billfishes, but with plenty of stamina as well.

TACKLE AND BAITS: Light ocean trolling or heavy spinning outfits with lines up to 30-pound test; 12- and 20-pound lines are tops for sport. Anglers targeting White Marlin usually choose rigged trolling baits, such as Ballyhoo, strips or squid. They will, of course, eagerly strike live Blue Runners, Goggle-eyes and similar baitfish that are considered standard Sailfish baits. Artificial trolling lures also take many Whites.

FISHING SYSTEMS: Trolling; sometimes Drifting.

Hatchet Marlin

Tetrapturus sp.

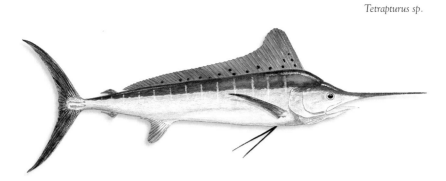

DESCRIPTION: The Hatchet Marlin may simply be a variant of the White Marlin, but a difference in the scales lends credence to the belief that it might be a distinct species. The scales are round, whereas those of the other Marlins are pointed. Coloration is similar to the other Marlins, but closer to the White than to the Blue in body proportions. The name comes from the dorsal fin, which does not dip in the manner of the Blue and White, but tapers gradually to the rear, outlining a fin that's intermediate in size between those of the other Marlins and the Sailfish.

SIZE: Uncertain; possibly to 200 pounds or more.

FOOD VALUE: If you catch one, save it for science!

GAME QUALITIES: Probably same as the White.

TACKLE AND BAITS: See White Marlin or Sailfish.

FISHING SYSTEMS: Trolling.

RANGE: *Rare everywhere. The few examples have come mostly from the Gulf of Mexico, but at least one suspected Hatchet Marlin was caught off Dade County and others have been reported in past years from Cuba. If it is truly a species, it probably occurs wherever Atlantic Marlins are found.*

HABITAT: *The open seas.*

Longbill Spearfish

Tetrapturus pfluegeri

Atlantic Spearfish

RANGE: *Deep waters off all Florida coasts, plus the Bahamas and Caribbean. Not common anywhere.*

HABITAT: *The open sea.*

DESCRIPTION: The name "Longbill" relates only to other Spearfishes occurring in different areas. Actually, the bill is quite short when compared to that of the Sailfish or White Marlin. Color usually is navy blue above; silvery on the sides and underparts. The dorsal fin is pointed at the front but dips only slightly and remains high for its full length—although not nearly high enough to mistake this species for a Sailfish.

SIZE: Usually 20-40 pounds; may reach 75 or more. World record 127 pounds, 13 ounces; Florida record 61 pounds, 8 ounces.

FOOD VALUE: Probably good but should be released.

GAME QUALITIES: Similar to Sailfish.

TACKLE AND BAITS: See Sailfish and White Marlin. Spearfish cannot be targeted and most catches are incidental to those fisheries.

FISHING SYSTEMS: Trolling.

Sailfish

Istiophorus platypterus

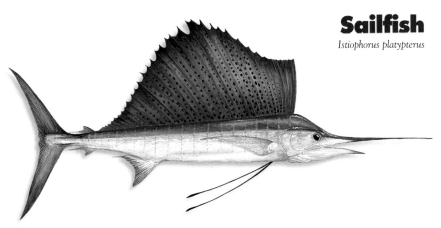

DESCRIPTION: Upper surfaces usually dark blue to black; silvery below; vertical stripes often visible on sides.

SIZE: Averages 30-60 pounds, but many under 30 pounds and a few up to 100 pounds are also taken. Potential maximum is less than 150 pounds in the Atlantic Ocean. World record 221 pounds; Florida record 116 pounds.

FOOD VALUE: Very good broiled or smoked, and should be kept if inadvertently killed. Protected commercially.

GAME QUALITIES: Unsurpassed in its size range for combined strength and spectacle.

TACKLE AND BAITS: Light ocean trolling or heavy spinning outfits with lines up to 30-pound test; 12- and 20-pound lines are adequate in experienced hands and provide great sport. In Southeast Florida, live-baiting—either by kite fishing or flatline drifting—has become perhaps the most popular approach to sailfishing, with Blue Runners, Goggle-eyes, Pilchards or Pinfish being the common offerings. Historically, most Sailfishing has been done with rigged trolling baits, mainly Ballyhoo and strips of Bonito or other small fish. Many Sailfish have been caught on jigs and on drifted Ballyhoo/jig combinations. Fly casters have also taken them on occasion, but Atlantic sails do not decoy as readily as their Pacific counterparts and so fly fishing for them has not become very popular—despite the fact that science has proclaimed the Sailfish of both oceans to be the same species.

FISHING SYSTEMS: Trolling; Drifting; occasionally Casting.

OTHER NAMES:
Atlantic Sailfish
Spindlebeak
Pez Vela

RANGE: All Florida coasts; Bahamas; Caribbean Islands. Most plentiful along Florida's Atlantic side from roughly Fort Pierce through the Keys.

HABITAT: Like the other Billfishes, the Sailfish is considered an ocean species, but generally can be found closer to land than the rest, seeming to prefer areas where coral reefs and/or freshwater runoffs mingle with ocean water. At times, particularly in Southeast Florida, the Sailfish comes right into the surf and quite a few have been caught over the years from beaches and piers.

Yes, Tunas actually are members of the Mackerel family, and the largest Tuna of them all—the Giant Bluefin—is called "Horse Mackerel" in parts of its range. Some members of this family—the Wahoo and most of the Tunas—are true pelagics that roam the open sea in the fashion of Marlin and Dolphin. Other members—the Mackerels and Little Tunny, for example, are called coastal pelagics because they do roam the seas, often migrating long distances, but generally stick fairly close to land. It is never surprising to encounter a coastal pelagic anywhere from the beach to deep blue water. True pelagics, on the other hand, stick to the deep blue—perhaps straying from it briefly now and then in the hunt for food. As a family, nearly all these fish rank high in angler esteem, the large Tunas being among the elite of big-game fishes, while the Mackerels and smaller Tunas provide some of the best sport available to shorebound anglers and small-boat fishermen.

Mackerels and Tunas

Wahoo

King Mackerel

Spanish Mackerel

Cero

Frigate Mackerel

Bluefin Tuna

Yellowfin Tuna

Blackfin Tuna

Little Tunny

Atlantic Bonito

Albacore

Skipjack Tuna

Bigeye Tuna

Wahoo

Acanthocybium solandri

OTHER NAMES:

Peto

Ono

RANGE: *Offshore of all Florida coasts, especially the Keys, but far more plentiful in the Bahamas and many Caribbean Islands.*

HABITAT: *Roams the deep blue water, but anglers can find them by working dropoffs, seamounts, weedlines and other favorable feeding locations.*

DESCRIPTION: Long, slender body marked with zebra-like stripes of white and deep blue or black. Mouth is elongated and narrow, and equipped with razor-sharp teeth—careful!

SIZE: Common at 10-50 pounds; often grows to 80 or 90 pounds; maximum potential about 150 pounds. World record 184 pounds; Florida record 139 pounds.

FOOD VALUE: White meat is tasty but rather dry. A good smoking fish.

GAME QUALITIES: May strike a surface bait in spectacular, greyhounding fashion, but seldom jumps after being hooked. Wild fight is characterized by several sizzling runs, usually at or near the surface. One of the fastest of all gamefish.

TACKLE AND BAITS: Many Wahoo are hooked on heavy tackle, incidentally to Billfishing. Best choices, however, are light to medium ocean trolling outfits with lines up to 30-pound test; 50-pound isn't too heavy for good sport with big specimens. A few have been caught by deepjigging or ocean casting with spinning and baitcasting tackle—even fly tackle on rare occasion. Most productive bait is a weighted feather or similar trolling lure, rigged in combination with a whole small baitfish or large strip. Surface trolling is sometimes effective, but deep trolling is much more likely to produce a Wahoo.

FISHING SYSTEMS: Trolling; Drifting.

King Mackerel

Scomberomorus cavalla

DESCRIPTION: Adults are heavy bodied, with large mouth and razor teeth. Elongated body is greenish above but mostly silvery and unmarked, except in juveniles, which have spots.

SIZE: School fish may run from 4 to around 20 pounds; individuals to 50 pounds, or slightly more, are not rare. Potential is from 75 to possibly 100 pounds. World record 93 pounds; Florida record 90 pounds.

FOOD VALUE: Depends on taste of the individual. Flesh is rich and oily. Fine broiled or smoked.

GAME QUALITIES: Kings are about as fast as Wahoo, although they seldom get that acknowledgment. Regardless, they are strong and sizzling fighters at any size.

TACKLE AND BAITS: Trollers generally choose ocean outfits with lines testing from 20-40 pounds, but kings of all sizes can be caught on spinning, baitcasting and even fly tackle. Spoons trolled behind planers are good, as are rigged Cigar Minnows and feather-minnow combinations. Fishing with Pilchards as both chum and live bait could be the most productive system of all, but drifting with rigged baits, strips or live baits, including live shrimp, is effective too. For casters, spoons and nylon jigs usually work best. Fly rodders do well with shiny flies on sinking lines.

FISHING SYSTEMS: Drifting; Trolling; Still Fishing.

OTHER NAMES:
Kingfish
Sierra
Cavalla

RANGE: All Florida coasts; also the Bahamas and Greater Antilles, but not in such great quantity.

HABITAT: In the Bahamas, around reef dropoffs. In Florida, widely distributed from the edge of blue water all the way to the beaches. Runs of schooling fish occur on both coasts in spring and fall, with action possible throughout the summer in North and Central Florida and, throughout the winter in Southeast Florida and the Keys. The runs take place, usually, in water from 20 to 100 feet deep, which is fairly close to shore along the Southeast Coast; farther out elsewhere. The very biggest fish, however, are often hooked very close in and are referred to as "Beachcombers."

Spanish Mackerel

Scomberomorus maculatus

OTHER NAMES:

Sierra

RANGE: *All Florida coasts, Cuba and Hispaniola; not present in most Caribbean Islands or the Bahamas.*

HABITAT: *Largely coastal, but roams offshore at times.*

DESCRIPTION: Dark above with silvery sides. Many spots, which are both yellow and brown. The body is proportionately deeper than with juvenile King Mackerel, and the yellow spots appear rounder and brighter, but if in doubt, the only true identifier is the lateral line, which tapers rather gently from front to back with no severe dip.

SIZE: Common at 1-3 pounds; not too unusual at 5-7 pounds; maximum potential over 10 pounds. World record 13 pounds; Florida record 12 pounds.

FOOD VALUE: If you like rich, rather dark fillets, they are great broiled or skinned and fried. Good smoked, too.

GAME QUALITIES: Outstanding on light tackle; very fast runs.

TACKLE AND BAITS: Spinning, baitcasting and fly outfits. Spinning is often best because the faster retrieve of a spinning reel is sometimes needed to move a lure at a pace that will interest the Mackerel. Best lures are small white nylon jigs and silver spoons, but many others work, including topwater at times. Flies should be small with lots of flash. Best baits are small silvery baitfish, live shrimp and drifted strips.

FISHING SYSTEMS: Drifting; Trolling; Still Fishing.

Cero

Scomberomorus regalis

DESCRIPTION: Similar to the Spanish Mackerel, except that the marks take the form both of spots and of broken lines.

SIZE: Averages 1-5 pounds, but 10-pounders are not rare, and the maximum approaches 20 pounds. World record 17 pounds, 2 ounces; Florida record 17 pounds, 2 ounces.

FOOD VALUE: Very good. Lighter flesh than the Spanish Mackerel, but nearly as oily.

GAME QUALITIES: Outstanding; very fast runs.

TACKLE AND BAITS: Spinning, baitcasting and fly outfits. Spinning is often best because the faster retrieve of a spinning reel is sometimes needed to move a lure at a pace that will interest the Mackerel. Best lures are small white nylon jigs and silver spoons, but many others work, including topwaters at times. Flies should be small and with lots of flash. Best baits are small silvery baitfish, live shrimp and drifted strips.

FISHING SYSTEMS: Drifting; Trolling; Still Fishing.

OTHER NAMES:

Cero Mackerel
Painted
   Mackerel
Sierra
   Pintada

RANGE: *This is the common mackerel of the Bahamas and Caribbean Islands. Also plentiful seasonally in the Florida Keys and Southeast Florida. Straggles to other Florida areas.*

HABITAT: *Coral reefs and inshore patches and shoals. Ventures to deep blue water as well.*

Frigate Mackerel

Auxis thazard

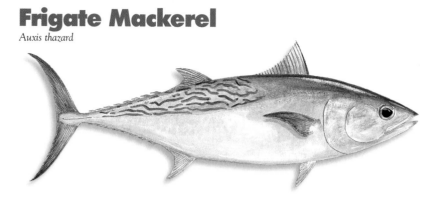

OTHER NAMES:

Bonito

Tinker Mackerel

RANGE: *Individually uncertain, but one or the other occurs throughout Florida, the Bahamas and the Caribbean.*

HABITAT: *The open sea, but often near deeper reefs.*

DESCRIPTION: The Frigate Mackerel, shown here, and the **Bullet Mackerel,** *Auxis rochei,* are two similar species confused by scientists and unrecognized by many anglers, who generally pass them off as juvenile Little Tunny. They do have the wavy lines of Little Tunny on the posterior dorsal area, and one of the species also has dots under the pectoral fin as the Little Tunny does. The anterior and posterior dorsal fins are widely separated, however, on the Frigate Mackerel, and nearly touching on the Little Tunny. Another smaller member of the clan is the **Chub Mackerel,** *Scomber japonicus,* also known as Tinker Mackerel, distinguished by black spots along the side.

SIZE: Averages about 12 inches; may reach 20 or 24. World record 3 pounds, 1 ounce.

FOOD VALUE: Seldom eaten because of a general prejudice against eating "Bonitos" of any sort. Indeed, the flesh is dark but not bad when boiled and made into Tuna salad.

GAME QUALITIES: Like other species of Tuna, they rank among the best battlers in their size group, mixing fast, zippy runs with as much pulling power as their small size allows.

TACKLE AND BAITS: When targeted (usually as bait for larger fish), the best outfit is a spinning rig with a small jig.

FISHING SYSTEMS: Trolling.

Bluefin Tuna

Thunnus thynnus

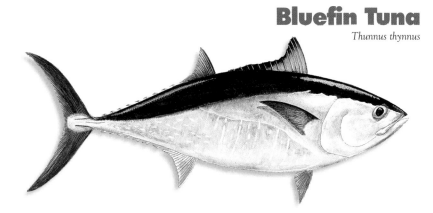

DESCRIPTION: The best identifier is huge size, since small Bluefins have always been almost non-existent in Florida and the tropics. The massive body is dark blue above, shading to silvery on the lower sides. All fins and finlets are steely blue.

SIZE: In the past, runs in the Bahamas (and, unpredictably, in Florida waters) consisted of fish weighing from about 200 to 600 pounds. Presently, most run over 500 pounds and many push 900. The increase in average size is indicative of the declining stock. Giant Bluefins are in trouble worldwide. World record 1,496 pounds.

FOOD VALUE: Too good for its own good. The Giant Bluefin is one of the most desired species in Japan, and in sushi bars worldwide. Also excellent when cut into steaks and broiled.

GAME QUALITIES: This is the toughest of all big-game fish to fight and land; has size, speed and stamina in boundless quantity. In classic Tuna fishing, the searching, chasing and baiting of the Tuna schools was as exciting as the fight, if not as punishing.

TACKLE AND BAITS: Heaviest sporting outfits with lines testing 80 or 130 pounds. Rigged swimming baits, such as large Mullet or Mackerel, or same baits in combination with large feathers. Also, offshore trolling lures.

FISHING SYSTEMS: Trolling (by sight, if possible; blind-trolling in desperation).

OTHER NAMES:

Giant Tuna
Horse Mackerel

RANGE: Historically, both sides of the Bahamas, plus Gulf of Mexico and, sporadically, the Caribbean. Occasional wayward schools would sweep past Southeast Florida in past years. Now scarce everywhere, a sport-fishery still exists in the Bahamas, primarily around Cat Cay and Bimini, but it is paltry compared to the years before commercial fishing ruined the stocks.

HABITAT: The deep sea.

Yellowfin Tuna

Thunnus albacares

OTHER NAMES:
Allison Tuna
Ahi

RANGE: All Florida, the Bahamas and the Caribbean.

HABITAT: The open sea, but frequently near dropoffs.

DESCRIPTION: Distinguishing the Yellowfin Tuna from the Blackfin or Bigeye is sometimes difficult as many visual features are similar. Finlets of the Yellowfin are yellow, trimmed in black. Gold stripe along side. Light underside usually shows spots and/or wavy lines. Second dorsal and anal fins of very large individuals are elongated and lunate—a feature not found on any other Tuna.

SIZE: May run anywhere from a few pounds to more than 200 pounds. Maximum close to 400. World record 388 pounds, 12 ounces; Florida record 240 pounds.

FOOD VALUE: One of the best.

GAME QUALITIES: Second only to Bluefin Tuna, and only because of smaller size.

TACKLE AND BAITS: Heavy outfits are indicated—50- or 80-pound. But light and medium ocean outfits are often used. Most are probably caught trolling with offshore trolling lures or rigged baits, but in certain areas the best approach is to anchor on a reef near deep blue water and bring in the fish by chumming with Pilchards or similar small baitfish. In that situation they can also be hooked by casting artificial lures with spinning, baitcasting and fly tackle—and landed, if the size is right and luck is with the angler.

FISHING SYSTEMS: Trolling; Still Fishing; Drifting.

Blackfin Tuna

Thunnus atlanticus

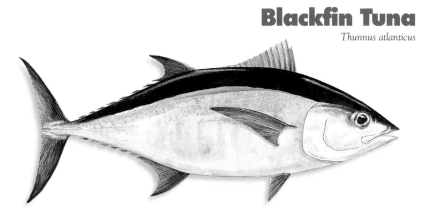

DESCRIPTION: Dark overall but with a bronze stripe down the side that can cause confusion with the more golden stripe of the Yellowfin Tuna. The finlets, however, are dark.

SIZE: Common from 2 to 20 pounds; exceeds 40 pounds. World and Florida records 49 pounds, 6 ounces.

FOOD VALUE: Excellent.

GAME QUALITIES: Pound-for-pound, among the best.

TACKLE AND BAITS: Light classes of ocean tackle, plus spinning and baitcasting outfits. For trolling, choose small offshore lures, feathers, spoons, small rigged baits such as Ballyhoo and strips. Deep-diving plugs are also good. Blackfins also can be chummed with live Pilchards or similar small baitfish, and fished for with the same bait, or by casting. Best hard lures are white jigs, tied with bucktail or feathers to provide a larger profile. Flies should be similarly tied—to imitate size and color of the live chum.

FISHING SYSTEMS: Trolling; Drifting; Still Fishing.

OTHER NAMES:
Bermuda Tuna
Football

RANGE: *All Florida, the Bahamas and Caribbean.*

HABITAT: *The open sea.*

Little Tunny

Euthynnus alletteratus

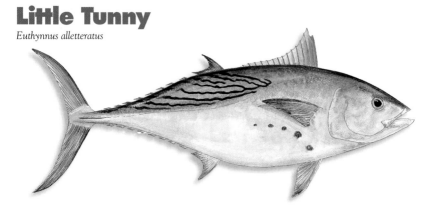

OTHER NAMES:
Blue Bonito
False Albacore
Little Tuna

RANGE: All Florida coasts, the Bahamas and the Caribbean.

HABITAT: A roamer, from close ashore to the deep sea.

DESCRIPTION: Wavy lines on back and spots around pectoral fin make this one easy to identify—but it is well known anyway to nearly every angler who ventures very far from shore.

SIZE: Common anywhere from a couple of pounds to 15 pounds; exceeds 30 pounds. World record 35 pounds, 2 ounces; Florida record 27 pounds.

FOOD VALUE: Not highly valued in Florida, but very good when lighter meat is separated from the darker.

GAME QUALITIES: Outstanding battler on light tackle.

TACKLE AND BAITS: Schools can often be approached and cast to with jigs, spoons and small plugs. They can be moody and selective, however, so you may have to try various baits and retrieves. Also a good fish for fly casters—with same advice. Often caught from piers on the Atlantic Coast and Panhandle, usually with tackle of surf dimensions. Trollers take them on everything from offshore lures and rigged Ballyhoo or Cigar Minnows to small feathers.

FISHING SYSTEMS: Drifting; Trolling.

Atlantic Bonito

Sarda sarda

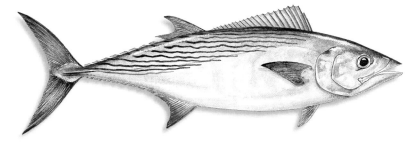

DESCRIPTION: Differs from Little Tunny (previous) in having a series of wavy lines along upper half of body, and no spots on lower half. Additionally, its two dorsal fins are not divided.

SIZE: Averages 4-10 pounds; maximum is possibly 20. World record 18 pounds, 4 ounces.

FOOD VALUE: Not well regarded but good.

GAME QUALITIES: Like other Tunas, an excellent fighter.

TACKLE AND BAITS: Usually overmatched with ocean trolling gear, but a great target, when the opportunity arises, for light casting tackle. Eagerly hits spoons, jigs and streamer flies, and also live fish and strip baits.

FISHING SYSTEMS: Trolling; Drifting; Casting.

OTHER NAMES:
Northern Bonito
Katonotel
Boston Mackerel

RANGE: A temperate species, not common in most of Florida but often seen along both the upper Atlantic and Gulf Coasts.

HABITAT: The open sea, but roams to the beaches.

Albacore
Thunnus alalunga

OTHER NAMES:
Longfin Tuna

RANGE: *Sometimes caught in deep waters off the Florida Gulf and Northern Atlantic Coasts. Said to occur throughout the tropics, but is nevertheless also uncommon in the Bahamas and Caribbean. Obviously prefers cooler waters.*

HABITAT: *The open sea.*

DESCRIPTION: The easiest Tuna to identify because of its extra-long pectoral fins, and because the trailing edge of the tail is white. Unfortunately, these indicators are seldom put to use in this area, where the Albacore is the rarest Tuna.

SIZE: Usually 10-50 pounds; sometimes exceeds 80. World record 88 pounds, 2 ounces.

FOOD VALUE: White, relatively tasteless flesh makes it less of a treat than other Tunas, although it's priced higher when bought from supermarkets in cans.

GAME QUALITIES: An outstanding battler, even among the hard-fighting Tuna clan.

TACKLE AND BAITS: Same as for Blackfins.

FISHING SYSTEMS: Trolling.

Skipjack Tuna
Katsuwonus pelamis

OTHER NAMES:
Oceanic Bonito
Arctic Bonito
Striped Tuna
Watermelon

RANGE: *All Florida coasts, the Bahamas and the Caribbean.*

HABITAT: *The deep sea.*

DESCRIPTION: Horizontal stripes on lower half of body distinguishes it from others of its clan.

SIZE: Common at 2-10 pounds; often exceeds 15 pounds. World record 45 pounds, 4 ounces; Florida record 33 pounds, 8 ounces.

FOOD VALUE: Dark flesh; good but not to most tastes.

GAME QUALITIES: A terrific light-tackle battler.

TACKLE AND BAITS: Any kind of casting tackle, small jigs, plugs and flies. If trolling, small feathers and spoons are best.

FISHING SYSTEMS: Trolling; Drifting.

Bigeye Tuna

Thunnus obesus

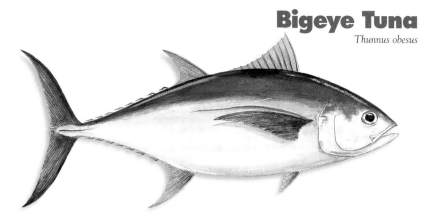

DESCRIPTION: Confusingly similar in looks to the Yellowfin Tuna—even down to the yellow finlets edged in black. The gold stripe common to the Yellowfin is usually absent, but may be dimly present. The eye is indeed larger, but this might not be readily apparent without a side-by-side comparison. A scientist might have to examine the liver to be perfectly sure of identification with some specimens, but anglers seldom have to worry, simply because the Bigeye is a rare catch, whereas the Yellowfin is common in many areas.

SIZE: About the same range as the Yellowfin—from a few pounds to more than 300, but most taken off Florida have run 50-100 pounds. World record 435 pounds; Florida record 167 pounds.

FOOD VALUE: Excellent.

GAME QUALITIES: A good-sized Tuna. Enough said.

TACKLE AND BAITS: Not targeted but sometimes hits trolled lures or shows up in a chumline; see Yellowfin Tuna.

FISHING SYSTEMS: Trolling; Drifting; Still Fishing.

RANGE: Uncommon but present off all Florida coasts, the Bahamas and the Caribbean

HABITAT: The open sea. As the bigeye proves, it stays deep most of the time and so may not be as rare as the low number of angling encounters would indicate.

Hefty Sharks are the only really big fish that are available for the hooking by virtually any fisherman, anywhere in salt water, from boat or shore. In the past, Sharks were ignored or maligned by the majority of anglers, with only a few of the largest kinds being grudgingly granted the accolade of "gamefish." Finally, however, they seem to have gained widespread acceptance as worthy sporting adversaries, and also—the smaller specimens, anyway—as food. Not that large Sharks can't be eaten too, but it's a rare angler who wishes to wrestle a big one into the boat simply for culinary purposes. It goes without saying that Sharks of any species can be dangerous unless handled with the greatest care, and the larger the Shark, the greater the danger.

There are three main groups of sharks we will deal with here in Florida. The first is the Hammerheads. They look like creatures from outer space with their eyes located at either end of broad, flat heads. Three of these are common throughout warm waters, but the Smooth Hammerhead likes cooler temperatures and is only a seasonal visitor to Florida. The second group, known as Requiem Sharks, includes most of the species regularly encountered by anglers in our coverage area. Some are popular sporting targets and easily recognized, but sorting out the identity of others can be difficult for many fishermen. Our third group is made up of ocean-roaming Sharks that are often talked about, but not often seen by anglers, especially the Threshers, which comprise a separate family, while the Makos and Great White are in a family that's referred to as Mackerel Sharks, probably because of their fast-swimming capabilities. In our part of the world, the Shortfin Mako, although by no means common itself, is encountered far more often than any of the others in this bunch.

Great Hammerhead

Smooth Hammerhead

Scalloped Hammerhead

Bonnethead

Reef Shark

Tiger Shark

Blacktip Shark

Sandbar Shark

Dusky Shark

Bull Shark

Oceanic Whitetip Shark

Silky Shark

Spinner Shark

Lemon Shark

Atlantic Sharpnose Shark

Nurse Shark

Thresher Shark

Shortfin Mako

White Shark

Great Hammerhead

Sphyrna mokarran

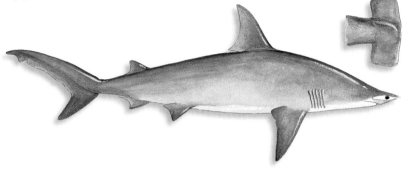

OTHER NAMES:
Giant
Hammerhead

RANGE: *All Florida, the Bahamas and the Caribbean.*

HABITAT: *The open sea. But often (too often?) ventures close to shore, and especially likes the deep Gulf Coast passes when schools of big tarpon are present.*

DESCRIPTION: Frequently identifiable by size alone. Small ones can be distinguished from the Scalloped Hammerhead by the rather flat frontal edge of the head, and by the rear edge of the pelvic fin, which is curved only in the Great Hammerhead.

SIZE: Commonly runs more than 500 pounds and sometimes as much as 1,000 pounds; possibly can reach one ton. Florida and world records 1280 pounds.

FOOD VALUE: Uncertain.

GAME QUALITIES: Monstrous size alone makes it an equally monstrous angling challenge.

TACKLE AND BAITS: Only the heaviest sporting gear stands much of a chance—130-pound line or, at the least, 80-pound. Will take a large fresh-dead baitfish, but is more easily hooked on oversize live bait.

FISHING SYSTEMS: Drifting; Still Fishing; Trolling.

Smooth Hammerhead

Sphyrna zygaena

DESCRIPTION: The head is very slightly rounded, but with no central indentation. Size and habits are similar to those of the Scalloped Hammerhead.

SIZE: Averages around 100 pounds; can top 200. World record 363 pounds.

FOOD VALUE: Good.

GAME QUALITIES: A voracious feeder that's usually easy to hook. Fight is fast and strong but not particularly long.

TACKLE AND BAITS: Like the Scalloped Hammerhead, it is a good candidate for lighter tackle, and takes the same baits.

FISHING SYSTEMS: Drifting; Still Fishing.

OTHER NAMES:
Common Hammerhead

RANGE: Appears on the East Coast of Florida during winter. Not found in the Bahamas or Caribbean.

HABITAT: The open sea, with forays into shallower water. Commonly seen at the surface by Atlantic offshore anglers.

Scalloped Hammerhead

Sphyrna lewini

DESCRIPTION: Slightly rounded frontal edge with several indentations, including one in center. Color is light brown above, shading to white on underside. Pectoral fin has a dark tip, but on underside only.

SIZE: Averages around 100 pounds; can reach 200 or more. World record 353 pounds.

FOOD VALUE: Good.

GAME QUALITIES: A voracious feeder that's usually easy to hook.

TACKLE AND BAITS: Live or fresh-dead baitfish will be the most eagerly accepted.

FISHING SYSTEMS: Drifting; Still Fishing.

RANGE: All Florida coasts, the Bahamas and Caribbean.

HABITAT: Open ocean, mostly, but commonly ventures close to the beaches and sometimes into large bays.

Bonnethead

Sphyrna tiburo

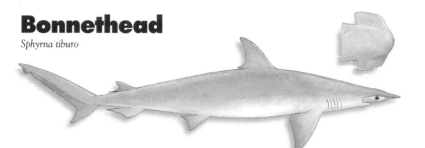

OTHER NAMES:

Bonnet Shark
Shovelnose Shark

RANGE: *All Florida coasts, the Bahamas and Caribbean.*

HABITAT: *Sticks largely to the shallows and is a common sight to the many Floridians who fish Speckled Trout and other species on the flats. Also roams channels and deeper water.*

DESCRIPTION: The Bonnethead is unmistakable because of its rounded or shovel-shaped head—not squared off or only slightly rounded as in the larger Hammerheads. Color is usually a very light gray, appearing almost white in the water.

SIZE: Averages 2-5 pounds; occasionally tops 10 pounds. World record 26 pounds.

FOOD VALUE: Good.

GAME QUALITIES: A spunky little fighter on light gear, but not so tough as other kinds.

TACKLE AND BAITS: Light spinning and baitcasting outfits. Any sort of small live fish or cut bait.

FISHING SYSTEMS: Drifting; Still Fishing.

Reef Shark

Carcharhinus perezi

OTHER NAMES:

Caribbean Reef
Shark

RANGE: *Probably the most familiar shark in shallow waters of the Bahamas and Caribbean; also plentiful in most areas of Florida.*

HABITAT: *Found w*
blue water to coastal water

DESCRIPTION: Gray or tan above, yellowish below. Tough to distinguish from the Dusky Shark, but the body is fatter, the gill slits smaller, and the trailing edge of the ventral fin is indented.

SIZE: Averages 10-30 pounds; seldom reaches 100. World record 154 pounds.

FOOD VALUE: Good.

GAME QUALITIES: Pretty good fighter, but usually small and seldom welcomed by anglers.

TACKLE AND BAITS: Spinning, baitcasting and light ocean outfits. Small dead fish and cut baits.

FISHING SYSTEMS: Still Fishing; Drift Fishing.

Tiger Shark

Galeocerdo cuvier

DESCRIPTION: Easily recognized by its pattern—and often by sheer size. Color is dark above, yellowish below. On smaller specimens, the darker markings take the shape of spots—hence the name "Leopard." The big ones become "Tigers" as the spots grow and blend together into stripes. The patterns, however, do vary a great deal.

SIZE: This is the largest Shark likely to be encountered by Florida anglers. Quite a few 1,000-pounders have been taken in the state, and the species probably grows to a ton in weight. World record 1,785 pounds; Florida record 1,065 pounds.

FOOD VALUE: Small ones good.

GAME QUALITIES: Not rated particularly high among Sharks, but sheer size and strength make it a rugged foe.

TACKLE AND BAITS: The heaviest sporting outfits are required for adult Tigers. Although the Tiger Shark will eat virtually anything, including shellfish and mammals, particularly good baits are Stingray wings and live or dead fish, that are appropriate to the size Shark being sought—very big baits on occasion.

FISHING SYSTEMS: Still Fishing; Drifting.

OTHER NAMES:
Leopard Shark

RANGE: *All Florida coasts, the Bahamas and the Caribbean.*

HABITAT: *The open sea, primarily, but many—including some giants—come close to the beaches.*

Blacktip Shark

Carcharhinus limbatus

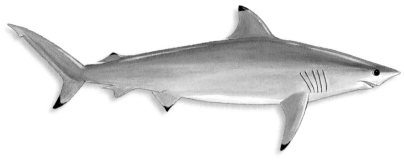

OTHER NAMES:
Small Blacktip

RANGE: *All Florida coasts, the Bahamas and the Caribbean.*

HABITAT: *Occurs from the open sea to the coast. One of the most familiar sharks in Florida, where it is often seen on shallow flats and along beaches and shorelines. Also plentiful around passes and inlets.*

DESCRIPTION: Gray above, white below. Tips of dorsal and pectoral fins are black, as is the lower lobe of the caudal fin. Short snout and stout body. Dorsal fin begins at a point above the rear portion of the pectoral fin.

SIZE: Common from 5-30 pounds; seldom reaches 100 pounds, but reported to 200 or more. World record 270 pounds, 9 ounces; Florida record 152 pounds.

FOOD VALUE: Very good.

GAME QUALITIES: Pound for pound, probably the scrappiest of sharks. Wages a wild battle on light tackle, marked by long runs and frantic jumps, especially in shallow water.

TACKLE AND BAITS: Spinning and baitcasting outfits; also fly outfits. Takes shrimp and any sort of fresh cut bait. With good presentation (Sharks have poor eyesight, and you have to put the lure very close to them), they will also hit a variety of artificial lures, especially topwater plugs and flyrod poppers; large (for purposes of visibility) streamer flies; slow-swimming jigs and underwater plugs.

FISHING SYSTEMS: Casting; Drifting; Still Fishing.

Sandbar Shark

Carcharhinus plumbeus

DESCRIPTION: Color ranges from gray to brown above, whitish below. Distinctive features are the wide, triangular dorsal and pectoral fins—with the dorsal situated almost directly above the pectoral.

SIZE: Averages 50-100 pounds; can exceed 250 pounds. World record 529 pounds.

FOOD VALUE: Good.

GAME QUALITIES: Not bad. Usually has enough heft to give the angler a good workout on medium tackle.

TACKLE AND BAITS: Heavy spinning and baitcasting; surf rods; light to medium ocean gear. Chunks of fresh-dead fish or Stingray wings make fine baits.

FISHING SYSTEMS: Still Fishing; Drifting.

OTHER NAMES:
Sand Shark
Brown Shark

RANGE: *All Florida coasts; less common in the Bahamas. Rare in most of the Caribbean.*

HABITAT: *Mostly inshore and around beaches; also in channels and other deeper areas. Doesn't mind murky water.*

Dusky Shark

Carcharhinus obscurus

DESCRIPTION: Dark gray above, shading to whitish below. Dorsal fin is triangular but not so broad as the Sandbar Shark, to which it is quite similar.

SIZE: Weighs up to 250 pounds. Maximum is probably around 500 pounds. Florida and world records 764 pounds.

FOOD VALUE: Good.

GAME QUALITIES: Strong and stubborn.

TACKLE AND BAITS: Medium to heavy ocean outfits; go lighter at your own risk. Any sort of fresh-dead fish or large fresh chunk of cut bait will work.

FISHING SYSTEMS: Still Fishing; Drift Fishing.

RANGE: *All Florida coasts; present, but not as numerous, in the Bahamas and Caribbean.*

HABITAT: *Primarily coastal, from beaches to deep reefs.*

Bull Shark

Carcharhinus leucas

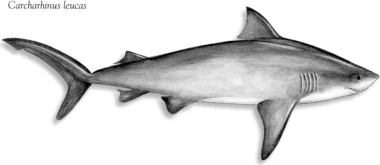

OTHER NAMES:

Ground Shark
Cub Shark

RANGE: *More common on all Florida coasts, but also occurs in the Bahamas and around larger islands of the Caribbean.*

HABITAT: *Primarily coastal. It also ventures into completely fresh water, and has been taken in several Florida rivers, and even in Lake Okeechobee.*

DESCRIPTION: Usually gray to light brown above, white below. Similar to the Sandbar Shark but has a shorter, wider snout. The large first dorsal fin starts above the middle of the pectoral fin, whereas in the Sandbar it starts above the front portion of the pectoral.

SIZE: Commonly runs 6-8 feet and 100-300 pounds, but can exceed 10 feet and 400 pounds. World record 697 pounds, 12 ounces; Florida record 517 pounds.

FOOD VALUE: Good.

GAME QUALITIES: A rugged fighter; usually has heft and strength on its side.

TACKLE AND BAITS: Although more appropriately matched to medium ocean outfits, the Bull is one of the pet targets of adventurous spin, plug and fly casters, especially in the lower Florida Keys. Will take a variety of dead fish as bait, and especially likes fresh-cut Barracuda. Also can be chummed into a mood for hitting artificials—large flies and topwater plugs being preferred.

FISHING SYSTEMS: Still Fishing; Drifting.

Oceanic Whitetip Shark

Carcharhinus longimanus

DESCRIPTION: Has white tips on the dorsal, pectoral and caudal fins. Even without the white (it's absent on a rare specimen) the high, rounded dorsal and long, rounded pectoral fins are giveaways.

SIZE: Up to 8-10 feet and 100-150 pounds. World record 369 pounds.

FOOD VALUE: Probably good.

GAME QUALITIES: An excellent battler on light-to-medium tackle.

TACKLE AND BAITS: Light to medium ocean tackle, with lines to 30-pound test. Sometimes a picky biter that insists on live bait; has been taken on cut baits.

FISHING SYSTEMS: Drifting; Trolling.

OTHER NAMES:
Whitetip

RANGE: Occurs on both sides of Florida in far offshore waters, but is far more often seen around the Bahamas and many Caribbean Islands.

HABITAT: Deep ocean only, but is occasionally encountered in areas where ocean depths closely approach island shores. In the Bahamas, it is common around certain deepwater manmade structures in the Tongue of the Ocean and Exuma Sound.

Silky Shark

Carcharhinus falciformis

DESCRIPTION: Gray to brown above, white below. Skin looks and feels silky. Dorsal is comparatively small and begins at a point behind the pectoral fin.

SIZE: Usually not very large—from 30-100 pounds—but is not rare at 200-300 pounds. World record 762 pounds, 12 ounces.

FOOD VALUE: Good.

GAME QUALITIES: Very good on suitable tackle.

TACKLE AND BAITS: Can often be sighted and—if the angler wishes—baited in clear offshore waters. Baits cut from fresh-dead fish, such as Bonito, are best.

FISHING SYSTEMS: Drift Fishing.

OTHER NAMES:
Wharf Shark

RANGE: All Florida coasts, the Bahamas and the Caribbean.

HABITAT: The open sea.

Spinner Shark
Carcharhinus brevipinna

OTHER NAMES:
Large Blacktip

RANGE: *All Florida coasts, the Bahamas, and the Caribbean.*

HABITAT: *The open sea; sometimes enters large inlets, particularly on the Florida East Coast.*

DESCRIPTION: Because of the black-tipped fins, many anglers think the Spinner and the Blacktip are one and the same. The Spinner is more slender in shape and has a longer snout. The dorsal fin begins at a point just aft of the pectoral fin.

SIZE: Common from 10-50 pounds; sometimes exceeds 100 pounds. World record 197 pounds, 12 ounces; Florida record 190 pounds.

FOOD VALUE: Very good.

GAME QUALITIES: Good fighter on light tackle; often gets off the high, spinning jumps that give it its name.

TACKLE AND BAITS: Medium to heavy spinning tackle and light ocean gear. Live Pilchards and similar baitfish are good choices. Fresh cut baits work pretty well.

FISHING SYSTEMS: Casting; Drifting; Still Fishing.

Lemon Shark
Negaprion brevirostris

OTHER NAMES:
Brown Shark

RANGE: *All Florida, the Bahamas and the Caribbean.*

HABITAT: *Forages a great deal over shallow flats and along shorelines; likes mouths of rivers and creeks. Spends time in deeper waters like channels and bays, but not far offshore, as a rule.*

DESCRIPTION: Brown with a yellowish cast to the underside. The first dorsal fin is short and not much larger than the second dorsal. The pectorals are triangular and wide.

SIZE: From around 20 pounds to well over 100 pounds. World record 405 pounds; Florida record 397 pounds.

FOOD VALUE: Good.

GAME QUALITIES: Less spectacular but otherwise pretty much the equal of the Blacktip as a light-tackle gamester.

TACKLE AND BAITS: Spinning and baitcasting outfits; also fly outfits. Will take a variety of live and dead natural baits and artificials.

FISHING SYSTEMS: Casting; Drifting; Still Fishing.

Atlantic Sharpnose Shark

Rhizoprionodon terraenovae

DESCRIPTION: The Atlantic Sharpnose shown here, and the **Caribbean Sharpnose**, *Rhizoprionodon porosus*, are identical in outward appearance. Color is brown or dark gray above; white below. Dorsal and caudal fins are edged in black.

SIZE: Averages 2 feet; maximum about 4 feet. World record 16 pounds.

FOOD VALUE: Very good.

GAME QUALITIES: Energetic and strong on light tackle.

TACKLE AND BAITS: Light tackle with wire leaders and small live or dead baitfish, or cut baits.

FISHING SYTEMS: Still Fishing; Drifting.

RANGE: *Science distinguishes this pair by a slight difference in bone structure. Anglers can distinguish them by range. The Atlantic Sharpnose is found throughout Florida; the Caribbean type in the Bahamas and Caribbean Islands.*

HABITAT: *Coastal, including surf, shallow flats and streams, often in schools.*

Nurse Shark

Ginglymostoma cirratum

DESCRIPTION: Overall brown or deep rust color. It has a very small, underslung mouth, and is our only Shark with barbels at the nostrils.

SIZE: Most seen in shallow water are from 5 to 50 pounds, but they can grow quite large in deeper water. World record 248 pounds.

FOOD VALUE: Excellent; probably the best of the Sharks, maybe because of its shellfish diet.

GAME QUALITIES: Probably the worst fighter of all the Sharks.

TACKLE AND BAITS: Anything goes except fly tackle. Although its natural diet is shellfish, it will eagerly take cut baits of any kind. Not fished with artificial lures.

FISHING SYSTEMS: Still Fishing.

RANGE: *All Florida coasts, the Bahamas and the Caribbean.*

HABITAT: *Frequently sighted on shallow flats of South Florida, the Bahamas and most Caribbean Islands, where it usually is lying still. Also lies still in deeper water around and under reefs, ledges and navigation markers.*

Thresher Shark

Alopias vulpinus

OTHER NAMES:
Fox Shark

RANGE: *All Florida, the Bahamas and Caribbean.*

HABITAT: *The deep sea; sometimes seen at the surface but almost always caught far under it.*

DESCRIPTION: The Thresher shown here, and the **Bigeye Thresher**, *Alopias superciliosus*, both have long, scythe-like tails.

SIZE: Average is 250-350 pounds; both grow to perhaps 1,000 pounds. World record 767 pounds, 3 ounces; Florida record 544 pounds, 8 ounces.

FOOD VALUE: Probably good, and the tail fin would make a lot of soup.

GAME QUALITIES: Said to be an excellent fighter.

TACKLE AND BAITS: Heavy classes of ocean tackle.

FISHING SYSTEMS: Drift Fishing.

Shortfin Mako

Isurus oxyrinchus

OTHER NAMES:
Bonito Shark
Blue Pointer

RANGE: *All Florida coasts; most often seen in Southeast Florida, the Bahamas and the Caribbean.*

HABITAT: *The open sea. Shortfin Makos frequently cruise, and strike at, the surface, whereas the Longfin is almost entirely a deep dweller.*

DESCRIPTION: The Shortfin Mako, shown here, is known to offshore anglers as, simply, "Mako." The **Longfin Mako**, *Isurus paucus*, is less often caught. Both have a huge mouthful of bulging teeth that are long and pointed. The Makos are blue above and white below.

SIZE: Range is 200-600 pounds, but both species can weigh more than 1,000 pounds. World record 1,221 pounds; Florida record 911 pounds, 12 ounces

FOOD VALUE: Excellent; comparable to Swordfish.

GAME QUALITIES: Considered by many big-game anglers as deserving of rank among the big Billfishes.

TACKLE AND BAITS: Ocean trolling tackle, in at least the 30-pound line class. Usually will strike rigged baits, such as Mullet and Mackerel, or a live Bonito.

FISHING SYSTEMS: Trolling; Drift Fishing.

The Rays

Southern Stingray

Largetooth Sawfish

Clearnose Skate

Southern Stingray

Dasyatis americana

OTHER NAMES:

Stingaree

Raya

RANGE: Commonly coastal, but Stingrays are also represented on and around coral reefs and even in the open sea.

HABITAT: Most species forage on soft bottom, particularly flats and shorelines.

DESCRIPTION: Several species are included under this collective name. They are dark colored and stand out vividly on shallow flats—unless buried in mud, which they often are while resting. The two most common in Florida are the pictured Southern Stingray, which grows the largest, and the **Atlantic Stingray**, *Dasyatis sabina*. In the Bahamas and throughout the Caribbean, the **Bluntnose Stingray**, *Dasyatis say,* is seen most often. All are flat and equipped with barbed spikes on their tails that can deliver a painful and possibly serious wound to an unwary wader, or to an angler who handles them carelessly.

SIZE: Usually 2-3 feet in "wingspan," although individuals can run at least twice that size. World record 246 pounds.

FOOD VALUE: Quite good; they do taste like scallops.

GAME QUALITIES: Not a great fighter, but strength and the tactic of sticking to the bottom like a suction cup can work up an angler's sweat. Stingrays can be the shallow-water angler's friend, however, since they create bright trails of silt when feeding, and these "muds" often attract gamefish, including Redfish, Jack, Snapper and even Bonefish.

TACKLE AND BAITS: All kinds of tackle. On the flats, try spinning tackle baited with shrimp or crab. From a pier or bridge, use heavier gear—maybe surf tackle—with the same sort of bait.

FISHING SYSTEMS: Still Fishing.

Largetooth Sawfish
Pristis pristis

DESCRIPTION: Brown or rusty in color; snout extends to a long, hard beak or "saw," fitted with sharp teeth on both sides. There is also a very similar species, the **Smalltooth Sawfish**, *Pristis pectinata*. Both are now pretty rare in Florida and the largetooth is encountered most often.

SIZE: Anglers are most apt to encounter small specimens, 2-6 feet long. World record 890 pounds, 8 ounces; Florida record 545 pounds.

FOOD VALUE: None. Protected species.

GAME QUALITIES: Poor, unless very large.

TACKLE AND BAITS: Seldom caught. Occasionally bites dead baits fished for Sharks.

FISHING SYSTEMS: Still Fishing.

RANGE: All Florida coasts. Some in the Greater Antilles. Rare in the Bahamas.

HABITAT: Likes mud or sand bottom along the coast, and will wander far up freshwater streams.

Clearnose Skate
Raja eglanteria

DESCRIPTION: Skates are flat like Stingrays, but generally have shorter, fatter tails and lack the dangerous spikes. Several species are taken in Florida—all equally disliked by anglers. The most common is the Clearnose, shown here, which has transparent "windowpanes" on either side of its pointed snout.

SIZE: Most types average about 18 inches in span, although some reach or exceed 3 feet.

FOOD VALUE: Good; same as Stingrays.

GAME QUALITIES: Poor.

TACKLE AND BAITS: Bottom tackle, with dead shrimp or cut bait.

FISHING SYSTEMS: Still Fishing.

RANGE: Common throughout Florida. Being coastal, Skates are not prominent in the Bahamas and Caribbean Islands.

HABITAT: Soft bottom near shore.

Mullets and Mojarras belong to different families but have many things in common—one being that several representatives of each family inhabit shallow, coastal water throughout Florida and the tropics, and often run into fresh water as well. Anglers in general concern themselves only with a couple of larger species in each group, paying less attention to the various small Mullets and Mojarras usually called "Shad" that are widely distributed but of virtually no angling importance.

Chapter

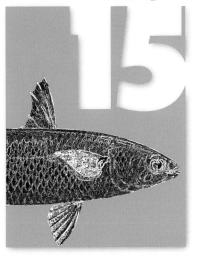

Mullets and Mojarras

Striped Mullet

White Mullet

Liza

Mountain Mullet

Irish Pompano

Yellowfin Mojarra

Striped Mullet "Black Mullet"

Mugil cephalus

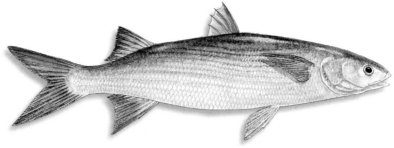

OTHER NAMES:
Jumping Mullet

RANGE: *All Florida coasts; absent from the Bahamas; not common in the Caribbean.*

HABITAT: *Most shallow coastal waters, and roams far into fresh water.*

DESCRIPTION: Head rounded; small mouth with rubbery lips; forked tail. Color is generally dark above—gray or brown—and white or light gray below. Longitudinal stripes generally quite noticeable.

SIZE: Averages 1-3 pounds, but this is the largest of the Mullets and can grow to at least 10 pounds on rare occasion. World record 7 pounds, 10 ounces.

FOOD VALUE: Excellent, both flesh and roe.

GAME QUALITIES: A zippy, frantic fighter.

TACKLE AND BAITS: A cast net is by far the best bet for catching Black Mullet, with the canepole a distant second. Mullet primarily feed on algae and do not bite in the usual sense. They will, however, take many small baits into their mouths briefly as they forage. Nearly all hook-and-line Mullet fishermen practice their art in freshwater streams or coastal canals. They mostly are canepolers who have the patience to stare at a float for extended periods, staying ready to heave at the slightest movement of the bobber, which indicates that a roaming Mullet is mouthing the bait. And baits are many indeed. They include bits of white plastic worm, real earthworms, corn, dabs of bacon and some other odds and ends. It's possible to catch Mullet by fly casting, but to do it you have to discover a situation in which the fish can be seen mouthing algae or other floating detritus at the surface. A fly of similar color, cast next to the floating stuff, is often taken in. But, like a canepoler, the fly fisherman must be constantly observant and ready to strike as soon as the take occurs; otherwise, the fly will be expelled.

FISHING SYSTEMS: Still Fishing.

White Mullet "Silver Mullet"

Mugil curema

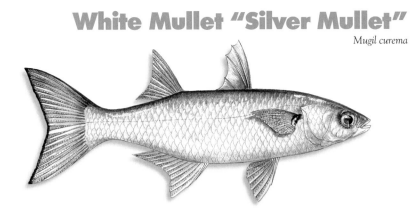

DESCRIPTION: Difficult to distinguish from the Black Mullet, especially if similar in size; however, the Silver Mullet is usually smaller, lighter in color and with less vivid stripes. The caudal fin of the Silver Mullet is edged in black, so that in the water, the tail looks as if it's marked with a black "V." The tail of the Black Mullet is dark overall.

SIZE: Averages a pound or less but can exceed three pounds. World record 1 pound, 7 ounces.

FOOD VALUE: Excellent, although most Silver Mullet end up as bait, not dinner.

GAME QUALITIES: Seldom caught on hook and line, but puts up a spirited fight, marked by wild jumps.

TACKLE AND BAITS: If you would fish for Silver Mullet with hook and line, the best spot to try would be around fish-cleaning tables. Watch for Mullet milling around. If any are spotted, use a tiny hook baited with a bit of entrail from cleaned fish, especially roe, if available. They are more easily hooked if you actually see them bite, since they generally suck in the bait and, just as quickly, eject it.

FISHING SYSTEMS: Still Fishing.

OTHER NAMES:
Lisa Blanca
Liseta

RANGE: All Florida. Although many in Florida think of the Black as the "Gulf Coast" Mullet, both are found on all coasts.

HABITAT: Shallow coastal waters. Enters fresh water, but less commonly than the Black Mullet.

Liza "Caribbean Mullet"

Mugil liza

OTHER NAMES:
Lisa

RANGE: *Bahamas and Caribbean; some in Florida.*

HABITAT: *Shallow shoreline areas.*

DESCRIPTION: Almost a dead ringer for the Black Mullet, but usually smaller and with a narrow, more pointed head.

SIZE: Common at 6-12 inches and grows to about 2 feet. World record 3 pounds, 3 ounces.

FOOD VALUE: Excellent.

GAME QUALITIES: Often seen; seldom hooked.

TACKLE AND BAITS: Nets.

FISHING SYSTEMS: Cast netting.

Mountain Mullet

Agonostomus monticola

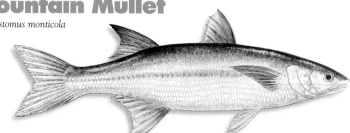

RANGE: *Occurs in Florida and throughout the Greater Antilles, but is prominent only in Jamaica, where a sport fishery exists in mountain streams.*

HABITAT: *Mostly in rivers, but also coastal. The Jamaica fishing is done at high elevation and in swift water.*

DESCRIPTION: Brown above, silvery below, with horizontal stripe on side. Tail is yellow.

SIZE: Usually less than a foot.

FOOD VALUE: Excellent.

GAME QUALITIES: Similar to small mountain trout.

TACKLE AND BAITS: Ultralight spinning and light fly outfits. Small spinners and a variety of wet flies work well. Pieces of avocado or other fruit are productive natural baits, as are kernels of corn.

FISHING SYSTEMS: Casting; Still Fishing.

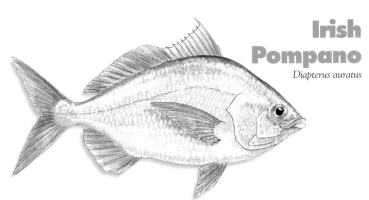

Irish Pompano

Diapterus auratus

DESCRIPTION: Body deep and compressed; second spine of dorsal and anal fins very long and strong. The mouth can be extended outward and downward. Color is greenish or grayish above, silvery below.

SIZE: Averages less than a pound.

FOOD VALUE: A good panfish.

GAME QUALITIES: Fun on light line.

TACKLE AND BAITS: Light or ultralight spinning outfits. Cut shrimp is best bait.

FISHING SYSTEMS: Still Fishing.

OTHER NAMES:
Mojarra
Shad
Punchmouth

RANGE: *Mostly found in the south half of Florida, both coasts.*

HABITAT: *Shallow water with mud or sand bottom. Likes quiet bays and coastal streams.*

Yellowfin Mojarra

Gerres cinereus

DESCRIPTION: Similar to the Irish Pompano in shape. Color brownish above, silvery below, with dark bars on the sides and yellow pelvic fins.

SIZE: Larger than the Irish Pompano. May top 1 pound. World and Florida records 1 pound, 3 ounces.

FOOD VALUE: A good panfish.

GAME QUALITIES: Spunky on light tackle.

TACKLE AND BAITS: Light spinning outfits, with bits of shrimp, clam or conch as bait.

FISHING SYSTEMS: Still Fishing.

OTHER NAMES:
Shad
Punchmouth

RANGE: *Mostly found in southern half of Florida, the Bahamas and the Caribbean.*

HABITAT: *Likes clear water of beaches, shorelines, shallow reefs and grass flats.*

A great many saltwater fish are capable of administering grievous wounds with teeth, spines or gill covers, but the following ones are especially dangerous, because they are so frequently encountered and—all too often— handled hastily and without due care. They are grouped together here mainly because most anglers consider every one of them a nuisance, even though both the Gafftopsail Catfish and Houndfish are sporty and good eating.

The Tooth and Spine Bunch

Hardhead Catfish

Gafftopsail Catfish

Gulf Toadfish

Needlefish

Houndfish

Inshore Lizardfish

Atlantic Cutlassfish

Hardhead Catfish

Arius felis

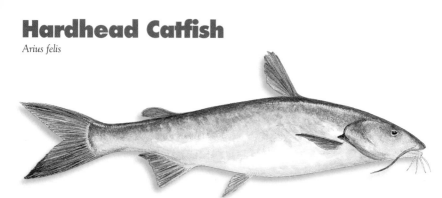

OTHER NAMES:

Marine Catfish
Sea Catfish
Seacat
Bagre

RANGE: All Florida coasts. Not found in the Bahamas; scattered in the Caribbean, mostly the large islands.

HABITAT: Lives anywhere in nearshore waters, but is most common in bays, harbors and coastal soft-bottom flats.

DESCRIPTION: Dingy gray on back and sides with white or silvery underside. Four fleshy barbels under the mouth and two more at corners of mouth. Forked tail. First spines of dorsal and pectoral fins are stiff and sharp and coated with venomous slime that can make a wound hurt for hours. Careful!

SIZE: Most run 1 pound or less, but may reach more than 4. World and Florida records 3 pounds, 5 ounces.

FOOD VALUE: Poorly regarded but pretty good.

GAME QUALITIES: Pulls pretty hard but gives up easily.

TACKLE AND BAITS: Any sort of light tackle will do—canepole, spinning or baitcasting. Eats shrimp and cut bait. Sometimes strikes artificial jigs and plugs.

FISHING SYSTEMS: Still Fishing; Drift Fishing.

Gafftopsail Catfish

Bagre marinus

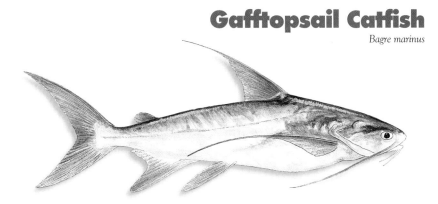

DESCRIPTION: Coloration is similar to the Common Cat, but the head is larger and wider. Most distinctive features are long, flowing extensions off the dorsal and pectoral fins, and very long barbels at the corners of the mouth. Only two barbels under the mouth. Thick slime makes the Gafftop difficult to handle, and the spines are as dangerous as those of the Marine Catfish.

SIZE: Averages more than a pound and is common at 2-4 pounds; maximum is around 8 pounds. World record 9 pounds, 10 ounces. Florida record 8 pounds, 14 ounces.

FOOD VALUE: Quite good. Has more of a table reputation than the Common Catfish.

GAME QUALITIES: Much tougher than the Common Catfish, and a willing striker on artificial lures.

TACKLE AND BAITS: Light spinning and baitcasting outfits. Like the Common Cat, will hit just about any dead bait, but prefers live bait and goes for many lures, including topwater plugs.

FISHING SYSTEMS: Still Fishing; Drifting; Casting.

OTHER NAMES:
Sail Cat
Schooner-Rig
Catfish
Joe Cat

RANGE: *Same as the Marine Catfish, but less common.*

HABITAT: *Coastal flats, channels and passes; also tidal streams. Found wherever the Common Catfish is found, but roams more widely throughout the water column in search of food.*

Gulf Toadfish

Opsanus beta

RANGE: *All Florida coasts.*

HABITAT: *Rocky areas, usually in shallow water.*

DESCRIPTION: The large, flat head and spiny dorsal fin and gill covers give the Toadfish a sinister look. Contrary to the belief of many fishermen, however, the Toadfish, though capable of administering minor hurts with its mouth and spines, is not venomous. The body is mottled brown and tan overall. The pectoral fins are large and rounded, and the tail is round as well. A smaller cousin, the **Oyster Toadfish,** *Opsanus tau,* is also encountered.

SIZE: Less than a foot long.

FOOD VALUE: Skip it.

GAME QUALITIES: Good strike; no pull.

TACKLE AND BAITS: Not targeted; usually caught by bottom fishermen using cut baits.

FISHING SYSTEMS: Still Fishing.

Needlefish

Strongylura sp.

DESCRIPTION: There are several species. All are nuisances to anglers. They are characterized by slender bodies and long, thin bills; both upper and lower beaks are equipped with many sharp teeth.

SIZE: Usually 1 foot or less; some reach 3 feet or so. World record 4 pounds, 1 ounce.

FOOD VALUE: Not bad, but not much meat.

GAME QUALITIES: Poor, despite a lot of thrashing.

TACKLE AND BAITS: Extra-light gear can provide some sport with extra-large Needlefish, but anglers generally try to avoid them. Needlefish will bite anything, and have a particular liking for small strips and bits of shrimp.

FISHING SYSTEMS: Still Fishing; Drifting.

OTHER NAMES:
Agujon

RANGE: All Florida coasts, the Bahamas and Caribbean.

HABITAT: Needlefishes seem to be everywhere, from the open sea to well up coastal streams into fresh water, always at the surface, and always on the alert for an un-weighted bait.

Houndfish

Tylosurus crocodilus

DESCRIPTION: Recognizable by the bars on its side near the tail, as well as by its bulk, compared to other Needlefishes. It poses more of a threat while jumping than while being handled. If one jumps close to the boat—duck!

SIZE: Averages a yard in length and can top 5 feet. World and Florida records 7 pounds, 8 ounces.

FOOD VALUE: Very good, but seldom eaten in Florida.

GAME QUALITIES: Wild fighter; spectacular jumper.

TACKLE AND BAITS: If targeting Houndfish, choose light spinning gear with small live baitfish or strip baits. A good fish for the fly rodder, too. Most catches, though, come incidentally to trolling.

FISHING SYSTEMS: Trolling; Drifting; Still Fishing.

OTHER NAMES:
Giant Needlefish
Guardfish
Agujon

RANGE: All Florida, the Bahamas and the Caribbean.

HABITAT: Common in the open seas, from reefs to blue water. Also found inshore, usually in areas of clear water and over deeper patches and grass beds.

Inshore Lizardfish

Synodus foetens

OTHER NAMES:
Galliwasp
Lagarto
Sand Pike

RANGE: The Offshore Lizardfish, along with other members of its family, is distributed throughout Florida, the Bahamas and the Caribbean. The Inshore Lizardfish is coastal.

HABITAT: Both types prefer soft bottom.

DESCRIPTION: There are several species, of which two are well known to many anglers—mostly as pests. The Inshore Lizardfish, shown here, and the **Offshore Lizardfish**, *Synodus poeyi*, are easy to distinguish, simply because one is caught in shallow coastal water and the other in deeper water farther offshore. Both are colored in shades of brown with dark blotches or diamond marks on the sides. The Offshore Lizardfish is usually more darkly colored and has a blunter head and even larger mouth than the inshore species, but both sets of jaws are wicked-looking and fitted with many sharp teeth.

SIZE: Paradoxically, the Offshore Lizardfish runs smaller, seldom reaching 1 foot, whereas the Inshore Lizardfish commonly exceeds that length and sometimes runs 15 or 16 inches. World record 2 pounds, 8 ounces.

FOOD VALUE: Not good; very bony.

GAME QUALITIES: Both types are vicious, persistent strikers, but too small to fight much.

TACKLE AND BAITS: Almost always caught while fishing for something else, Lizardfish strike any sort of live or dead bait and have no bias at all against artificial lures, at which they usually keep banging away until they finally get hooked.

FISHING SYSTEMS: Still Fishing; Drift Fishing.

Atlantic Cutlassfish

Trichiurus lepturus

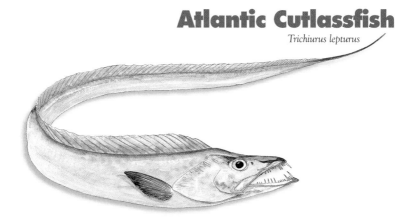

DESCRIPTION: The silver body is flat and ribbon-like, with a full-length dorsal fin but only a point where the "tail" should be. The wide mouth is well equipped with fang-like teeth that a Moray might envy, but the Cutlass is not particularly dangerous if handled with caution.

SIZE: Averages about 2 feet long; sometimes to 4 feet, but it is indeed ribbon-like in build and does not weigh much for its length. World record 8 pounds, 1 ounce.

FOOD VALUE: Forget it. Not much flesh, and very bony.

GAME QUALITIES: As lightweight a fighter as its build would indicate, the Ribbonfish never threatens to tear up your tackle.

TACKLE AND BAITS: Usually caught on tackle scaled for Mackerel and Bluefish. Will hit live baits, strip baits and a variety of artificial lures.

FISHING SYSTEMS: Still Fishing; Drifting; Trolling.

OTHER NAMES:
Ribbonfish
Silverfish

RANGE: All Florida coasts, the Bahamas and Caribbean.

HABITAT: Open water; enters bays, inlets and coastal streams, often in company with Spanish Mackerel or Bluefish. Most are probably caught by bridge fishermen seeking those species.

All the fish lumped in this chapter are oddities of one sort or another. Remoras are strange fish with sucker disks on top of their heads—an arrangement which allows them to glue themselves to larger hosts and ride along in hopes of dining on leftovers when the big boys feed. They swim freely as well and can hunt up their own food when necessary. Some are host-specific, meaning they stick to a particular type of animal, which, may be a mammal, a turtle or a particular type of big fish.

Only a couple of kinds are commonly caught by anglers, although others sometimes are. Puffers swell themselves up—in the water or out of it—as a defensive measure. Trunkfish have their skeletons at the surface. Searobins look like they belong in the air, not under water. Few of the fish in this section have much of an angler following, but all are caught with varying frequency, and some are good to eat, if frustrating to clean.

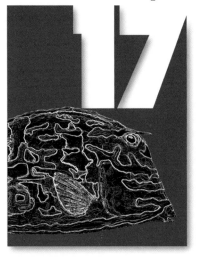

Hitchhikers, Blowhards and 'Whatzits'

Sharksucker

Remora

Southern Puffer

Scrawled Cowfish

Smooth Puffer

Bighead Searobin

Sharksucker

Echeneis naucrates

OTHER NAMES:
Remora

RANGE: *All Florida coasts, the Bahamas and the Caribbean Islands.*

HABITAT: *Free-roaming; offshore and inshore.*

DESCRIPTION: Color ranges from near black to gray, but always with a vivid white-bordered dark stripe the length of the side. In the water, this can cause a Sharksucker to be mistaken for a small Cobia.

SIZE: Usually 1 foot or less, but can exceed 3 feet. World record 5 pounds, 1 ounce.

FOOD VALUE: Not generally eaten.

GAME QUALITIES: Fights pretty well for its size, but has been known to cheat by grabbing an angler's bait, then quickly sticking itself to a much larger fish and letting the host wage the battle. Usually it comes loose, leaving the puzzled angler trying to figure out how a fish so small could pull like a submarine.

TACKLE AND BAITS: Not targeted. Caught on all sorts of gear and any kind of natural bait it can swallow.

FISHING SYSTEMS: Drift Fishing; Still Fishing.

Remora

Remora remora

OTHER NAMES:
Sharksucker

RANGE: *Florida, the Bahamas and the Caribbean.*

HABITAT: *Free-roaming; usually offshore.*

DESCRIPTION: Solid gray or charcoal all over; lacks the stripe of the preceding fish. Also rounder in shape and usually smaller. Caught far less often by anglers.

SIZE: From several inches to a couple of feet.

FOOD VALUE: Nil.

GAME QUALITIES: See Sharksucker.

TACKLE AND BAITS: See Sharksucker.

FISHING SYSTEMS: Drift Fishing; Still Fishing.

DESCRIPTION: Floridians may call any of several species of Puffers a Blowfish or Toadfish, but the three most commonly caught are the Southern Puffer, shown here, which wears circular markings, the **Checkered Puffer**, *Sphoeroides testudineus*, whose marks are leopard-like, and the **Bandtail Puffer**, *Sphoeroides spengleri,* which is just as its name states. All are mottled yellow or brown, approximately the same size, and have large, powerful clipping teeth that can nip a chunk out of a careless angler. Their bellies are rough when inflated. Two other puffer cousins, the **Striped Burrfish**, *Chilomycterus schoepfi*, and the **Porcupinefish**, *Diodon hystrix,* are adorned with sharp spikes.

SIZE: Averages less than a foot.

FOOD VALUE: The meat is delicious. Unfortunately, however, the entrails and skin contain a poison that has caused numerous fatalities with fish not properly cleaned. Skip them.

GAME QUALITIES: Not much.

TACKLE AND BAITS: As long-suffering inshore anglers know, Blowfish will hit many kinds of lures, generally ruining those made of plastic or hair. They will take any sort of natural bait as well, and the few people who go after them for food use small hooks baited with dabs of shrimp, squid or cut fish. No sport on any tackle.

FISHING SYSTEMS: Still Fishing; Drifting; Casting.

OTHER NAMES:
Blowfish
Tambor

RANGE: *Both of these as well as several less familiar types occur along all Florida coasts, and throughout the Bahamas and Caribbean.*

HABITAT: *The Puffers are widely at home in many shallow, coastal habitats.*

Scrawled Cowfish

Lactophrys quadricornis

RANGE: *All Florida coasts; more common in South Florida, the Bahamas and the Caribbean.*

HABITAT: *Shallow inshore areas with grassy bottom.*

DESCRIPTION: There are several familiar species, all of which wear their skeletons on the outside (covered by skin, of course) in the form of tank-like armor. Their mouths are small and the heads slope sharply. The Scrawled Cowfish is the most popular of the Boxfish, with other commonly seen relatives being the **Smooth Trunkfish**, *Lactophrys triqueter*, and the **Trunkfish**, *Lactophrys trigonus*.

SIZE: Usually a foot or less, but can exceed 18 inches.

FOOD VALUE: Said to have excellent meat inside its armor, but also said to be toxic at times. This is another one that the angler might as well skip.

GAME QUALITIES: Boxfish bite small natural baits but have little strength and less speed. Their chief contact with sport fishermen comes on the Bonefish flats of South Florida and the Keys, where they sometimes make great nuisances of themselves—like Blowfish—by attacking the angler's shrimp baits.

TACKLE AND BAITS: If you want to catch one, light spinning tackle with small hook and live or dead shrimp for bait would be the best approach.

FISHING SYSTEMS: Still Fishing.

Baitfishes

Ballyhoo

Bigeye Scad

Round Scad

Redtail Scad

Atlantic Menhaden

Scaled Sardine

Atlantic Thread Herring

Spanish Sardine

Bay Anchovy

Ballyhoo

Hemiramphus brasiliensis

OTHER NAMES:

'Hoo

Halfbeak

RANGE: *All Florida, Bahamas and Caribbean.*

HABITAT: *Most common around reefs and shoals, but widespread from deep water to larger bays.*

DESCRIPTION: Ballyhoo differ from the Needlefishes in that only the lower jaw of the 'Hoo is elongated into a "bill." Several species occur in our waters, but only two are prominent. Their ranges overlap and their appearance is so similar that few anglers care about distinguishing them. The ballyhoo, shown here, has a short pectoral fin and the upper lobe of its tail fin is gray. The **Balao**, *Hemiramphus balao*, has a long pectoral fin and the upper lobe of the tail is reddish.

SIZE: Both species average 10-12 inches, but commonly reach 15 or 16 inches.

FOOD VALUE: Not bad, but seldom eaten.

GAME QUALITIES: Cagey biters and zippy little fighters, but too small to merit attention except when bait is needed.

TACKLE AND BAITS: Ballyhoo respond readily to ground chum. Although cast netting is the way to capture more of them, they can be caught with tiny hooks and small bits of cut bait, fished from spinning outfits or poles.

FISHING SYSTEMS: Still Fishing.

Bigeye Scad "Goggle-eye"

Selar crumenophthalmus

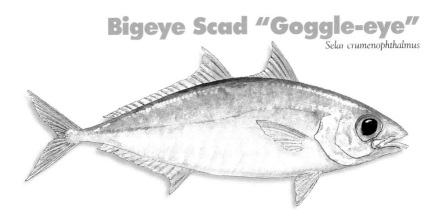

DESCRIPTION: Elongated, cylindrical body with forked tail. Scutes forward of tail. Color is steel blue above and on the sides; silvery below. Very large eye.

SIZE: Less than one foot.

FOOD VALUE: Good, but usually used for bait.

GAME QUALITIES: Like the rest of the Jack family, of which Scad are members, it is a great fighter for its size.

TACKLE AND BAITS: Most Goggle-eyes are caught at night, either deliberately as potential bait, or accidentally while chumming and bottom fishing. In either case, light spinning tackle is generally used. Bait fishermen tempt their Goggle-eyes with small jigs, often tied in tandem or series.

FISHING SYSTEMS: Still Fishing.

OTHER NAMES:

Gog
Goggle-eye Jack

RANGE: All Florida, Bahamas and Caribbean.

HABITAT: Reefs and other outside waters; also in and near inlets. May also enter larger bays and river mouths.

Round Scad "Cigar Minnow"

Decapterus punctatus

OTHER NAMES:

Hardtail

Cigarfish

Chuparaco

RANGE: All Florida, Bahamas and Caribbean.

HABITAT: Large schools are widespread in the Gulf and Atlantic, from near the beaches to well offshore.

DESCRIPTION: As the name suggests, the body is cigar-shaped. The tail is forked and scutes are present. Small black spots are present along the lateral line. Color is dull gray or tan with whitish underside.

SIZE: Under a foot; averages 6-8 inches.

FOOD VALUE: Used as bait, not food.

GAME QUALITIES: None.

TACKLE AND BAITS: Although anglers purchase most of their Cigar Minnows in fresh or frozen state, they can be caught on bait rigs—a series of tiny hooks that are sometimes dressed with nylon filaments, although Glass Minnows will just as readily take the plain hooks. This rig can be purchased at tackle shops or put together by the angler. A sinker is fixed to the end of the string of hooks. A stout rod and fairly heavy line will make things easier, since no sport is involved, and since the sinker may have to be rather heavy, depending on the depth at which the Cigar Minnows, spotted by sonar, are hanging.

FISHING SYSTEMS: Drifting; Still Fishing.

Redtail Scad "Speedo"

Decapterus tabl

DESCRIPTION: Cigar shaped. Scutes are present and tail fin is vivid red.

SIZE: Larger than Cigar Minnow; averages 12-14 inches.

FOOD VALUE: Edible but seldom put on the table.

GAME QUALITIES: Often a challenge to hook up, but no great shakes as a fighter because of small size.

TACKLE AND BAITS: To catch Speedos as bait for King Mackerel and other gamefish, try your lightest spinning outfit with hair hook and bits of ground chum as bait. If any is available, canned corn may be the best bait of all.

FISHING SYSTEMS: Still Fishing.

RANGE: All Florida, Bahamas and Caribbean.

HABITAT: Widespread on both coasts. Very commonly seen in chumlines in Southeast Florida and the Keys.

Atlantic Menhaden

Brevoortia tyrannus

Pogy
Mossbunker
Bunker
Alewife
LY
Fatback
Shad

RANGE: *All Florida.*

HABITAT: *All the Menhadens range widely in open water of the Gulf and Atlantic, but are most often sought by anglers fairly close to the beaches, or around shoals and wrecks.*

DESCRIPTION: Three species of Menhaden are common in Florida, but all are similar in size and appearance, and interchangeable in their bait appeal. The Atlantic Menhaden, shown here, is slightly larger than its Gulfside counterparts, the **Gulf Menhaden**, ***Brevoortia patronus***, and the **Yellowfin Menhaden**, ***Brevoortia smithi***. The latter two can be distinguished by their spots—a lone prominent spot behind the gill cover of the Yellowfin, as opposed to a large spot and a series of smaller ones on the Gulf Menhaden. The Atlantic variety also has numerous spots. All three have dark greenish backs, yellowish fins and dull silver or brassy sides.

SIZE: To about 12 inches. The average is about 8 inches.

FOOD VALUE: Very oily. Best used for bait and for sliced or ground chum.

GAME QUALITIES: The Menhadens are very strong and active for their size, which makes them ideal as bait for fast-swimming gamefish. They fight well on very light spinning tackle.

TACKLE AND BAITS: Most are cast netted, but many are caught on spinning tackle with multi-hook bait rigs.

FISHING SYSTEMS: Still Fishing; Drift Fishing.

Scaled Sardine "Pilchard"

Harengula jaguana

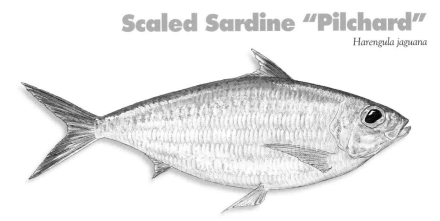

DESCRIPTION: Again, we have several similar species that most anglers make little or no attempt to differentiate, and which are known by various common names, mostly regional. Actually, it would be a surprise to find a listing under the name "Pilchard" in scientific books. The Scaled Sardine is the one most widely called "Pilchard," at least on the East Coast. The same fish (with some others) is usually called "Whitebait" in the Gulf. Color is usually brassy above and solid silver on sides. Small black spot may be present on the gill cover. The similar **Redear Sardine**, *Harengula humeralis,* and **False Pilchard**, *Harengula clupeola,* occur in South Florida but are less common. Both have an orange spot on the gill cover, but the False Pilchard is solid, whereas the Redear Sardine shows dark broken streaks on the upper sides.

SIZE: Averages 3-6 inches.

FOOD VALUE: Insignificant.

GAME QUALITIES: None.

TACKLE AND BAITS: Most are cast netted, but they can also be caught with either multi-hook bait rigs, or with "Pilchard rings"—a series of small, interlocking rings fashioned of leader wire. Both rigs are sold in bait shops in areas where they are popular. If the Pilchards are present but not densely packed, they are first chummed up with grain, such as oatmeal, and then the bait rigs or Pilchard rings are lowered into the school. The Pilchards either strike the hooks or swim into the rings, which trap them.

FISHING SYSTEMS: Still Fishing.

OTHER NAMES:
Whitebait
Sardina

RANGE: Florida and Bahamas.

HABITAT: Roams widely in both shallow and deep water of both coasts. Bait-seekers look for them inshore on grassy flats and around bridges. Offshore, they frequently congregate near navigation markers, wrecks and reefs.

Atlantic Thread Herring

Opisthonema oglinum

OTHER NAMES:
Greenie
Greenback
Shiner
Thread
Machuelo

RANGE: *Widespread in Florida.*

HABITAT: *Both inshore and off-shore waters.*

DESCRIPTION: Similar to the Pilchard but with a deeper body and larger eye. Also easily distinguished by the elongated, threadlike posterior ray of the dorsal fin. Dark spot behind gill cover.

SIZE: Averages 4-6 inches; maximum about 12 inches.

FOOD VALUE: Seldom eaten.

GAME QUALITIES: None.

TACKLE AND BAITS: Usually caught in cast nets, but also on multi-hook bait rigs.

FISHING SYSTEMS: Still Fishing.

Spanish Sardine

Sardinella aurita

OTHER NAMES:
Sardine
Shiner
Herring

RANGE: *Widespread, all areas.*

HABITAT: *Common on inshore flats, but occurs in deep water too.*

DESCRIPTION: Both the Spanish Sardine, shown here, and the **Orangespot Sardine**, *Sardinella brasiliensis*, are more elongated and less flattened than other Herrings. Silver sides and green back. Spanish has no markings, whereas Orangespot has a gold or light orange streak on the side.

SIZE: Averages 2-4 inches; reaches 10 inches or so. Orange Sardine usually is smaller than the Spanish.

FOOD VALUE: Good, but seldom eaten.

GAME QUALITIES: None.

TACKLE AND BAITS: Will respond to chum and can then be cast netted or taken on tiny hooks

FISHING SYSTEMS: Still Fishing.

Bay Anchovy "Glass Minnow"

Anchoa mitchilli

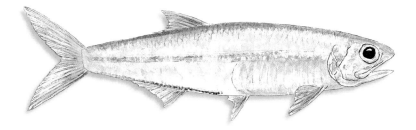

DESCRIPTION: Glass minnows are those little, transparent fish that can be seen just about anywhere in salt water—often in dense schools. The great majority of them are the Bay Anchovy, shown here, or the **Striped Anchovy**, *Anchoa hepsetus,* or the **Cuban Anchovy**, *Anchoa cubana*, although some schools of Glass Minnows might be a potpourri of species including, among others, tiny Herrings and even embryonic gamefishes. The Anchovies are characterized by a tiny underslung mouth.

SIZE: Average is 1 or 2 inches. None are likely to exceed 3 or 4 inches.

FOOD VALUE: As with canned Anchovies, edible but debatable.

GAME QUALITIES: None.

TACKLE AND BAITS: Beach seines; dip nets; cast nets.

FISHING SYSTEMS: Netting.

OTHER NAMES:

Fry
Bigmouth Fry
Anchoa

RANGE: *Anchovies of several species are found throughout Florida, the Bahamas and Caribbean—any or all of which may constitute the blocks of frozen Glass Minnows available in bait stores for use as chum or, sometimes, as bait.*

HABITAT: *Most are found in shallow water and along shorelines, but some occur far offshore.*

n the past, as many as five distinct kinds of Black Bass were said to inhabit parts of Florida—including the Smallmouth Bass and the Kentucky or Spotted Bass. Indeed, the Smallmouth world record was once listed as having been caught in the state. Scientists now agree that only the following three species are found in Florida, and that only the Largemouth lurks in the great majority of our bass waters. The Florida Largemouth is considered a subspecies apart from the Southern and Northern Largemouths. It eats more heartily, grows faster and averages larger than its upcountry cousins.

The Black Basses

Florida Largemouth Bass

Suwannee Bass

Redeye Bass

Florida Largemouth Bass

Micropterus salmoides floridanus

OTHER NAMES:
Black Bass
Green Bass
Bigmouth
Bucketmouth

RANGE: Statewide.

HABITAT: Varies with season and water temperature, but Largemouths of all sizes love cover—pads, grass, snags, docks, whatever. Younger, active fish often school in open water, chasing baitfish.

DESCRIPTION: Overall green in color, varying from light green to almost black. Often wears a dark stripe or interrupted stripe from gill cover to tail. Jaw (maxillary) extends beyond the eye. Note notch separating two sections of dorsal fin.

SIZE: Caught in all sizes from three or four inches long to 15 pounds or more. Usual maximum is 8-10 pounds. World record 22 pounds, 4 ounces; Florida record 17.27 pounds.

FOOD VALUE: Excellent in smaller fish. Large bass are more coarse and should be released anyway.

GAME QUALITIES: Aggressive striker; strong and acrobatic fighter. The Largemouth may not be the "gamest fish that swims"—as the old quotation goes—but it ranks among the best battlers in fresh water.

TACKLE AND BAITS: The most popular tackle for good-size bass in or near cover is a heavy baitcasting outfit with line ranging from 15-pound test to 30. Much lighter tackle can be used successfully in open water. Baits include weedless plastic worms, spinnerbaits, weedless spoons, topwater plugs and, in open water, swimming plugs. King of natural baits is the Golden Shiner, preferably native-bred and large. Chubs, Bream and Shad are also productive, as are large earthworms. Fly fishermen depend on large popping bugs and big streamer flies, often tied long and snaky to resemble worms or eels.

FISHING SYSTEMS: Casting; Trolling; Drifting.

Suwannee Bass

Micropterus notius

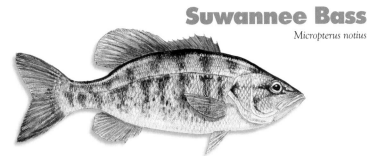

DESCRIPTION: Tan or gold background with numerous dark brown markings. Belly is silvery blue. Eye is red.

SIZE: Most run 1-2 pounds. World and Florida records 3 pounds, 14 ounces.

FOOD VALUE: Excellent.

GAME QUALITIES: Possibly even more aggressive than the Largemouth and tougher for its size.

TACKLE AND BAITS: Light spinning and baitcasting outfits. Best natural bait is a crawfish, but minnows and worms also produce. Lures include spinnerbaits, and lightweight topwater minnow plugs.

FISHING SYSTEMS: Still Fishing; Casting; Drifting.

RANGE: *The Suwannee River system and (less plentifully) the Ochlockonee River and its tributary creeks. Quite numerous in most of the Suwannee and its major tributary rivers.*

HABITAT: *Shares most waters with the Largemouth Bass but prefers swifter water and rocky bottom.*

Redeye Bass "Chipola Bass"

Micropterus coosae

DESCRIPTION: Light in color with a white underside. Dark spot at base of tail. Eye red.

SIZE: Common at 1-3 pounds. World record 8 pounds, 12 ounces; Florida record 7.83 pounds.

FOOD VALUE: Excellent.

GAME QUALITIES: A ready striker and spirited battler.

TACKLE AND BAITS: Light spinning and baitcasting outfits. Loves crawfish, but minnows and worms also produce. Favorites include spinnerbaits, topwater slender minnow plugs, plastic worms and small crankbaits.

FISHING SYSTEMS: Casting; Still Fishing; Drifting.

OTHER NAMES:
Shoal Bass

RANGE: *The Apalachicola River system of the Eastern Florida Panhandle; most often seen in the Chipola River, an Apalachicola tributary.*

HABITAT: *Prefers clear, running water with hard bottom, but also roams to other riverine habitats.*

"**S**unfish" is a label printed in books and spoken in many other states, but seldom heard in Florida, where many members of this large family are referred to collectively as Bream or Perch, and individually by more romantic or colorful names. Whatever you might care to call them, these panfish rank as the best-loved of Florida's freshwater fishes by anglers of all ages. The Largemouth and other Black Basses belong to this family as well, but are generally thought of in a different angling light, and so the two sub-groups have been allotted separate chapters here.

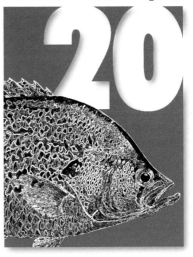

The Bream and 'Perch'

Black Crappie "Speckled Perch"

Pomoxis nigromaculatus

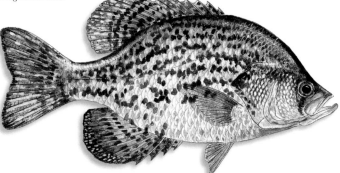

OTHER NAMES:

Crappie
Speck
Calico Bass

RANGE: Statewide.

HABITAT: Prefers calm and reasonably clear water. Generally stays deep, around brush or other structure, except during the spawning season of late winter and early spring, when it beds in water as shallow as 3-4 feet deep around grass or other aquatic vegetation. Found both in lakes and in rivers with deep, slow stretches of water.

DESCRIPTION: Dark gray or greenish on back, shading to silvery or white on sides. Sides marked with many spots and wavy, broken lines. Posterior dorsal and anal fins are large and fanlike. The very similar White Crappie is seldom found in Florida.

SIZE: The average is 8-12 ounces; specimens between 1-2 pounds are fairly common; maximum probably around 4 pounds. World record 5 pounds; Florida record 3.83 pounds.

FOOD VALUE: Excellent; white, fine-grained meat.

GAME QUALITIES: Fair; not as spunky as other panfish.

TACKLE AND BAITS: Nothing beats a canepole and "Missouri Minnows"—the name given to the small minnows sold in bait shops. Any sort of wild minnow or small baitfish will do, however. Grass shrimp are excellent too, and earthworms work to some extent. Ultralight and light spinning outfits rival the pole in productivity at times. Leading lures are tiny leadhead jigs and in-line spinners, small spinnerbaits and midget models of swimming plugs (crankbaits). Fly rodders pick up an occasional Speck on surface bugs while potluck fishing, but if targeting them, should cast small streamer flies with sinking lines. Flyrod spinners rank among the top choices.

FISHING SYSTEMS: Drifting; Still Fishing; Trolling; Casting.

Warmouth

Lepomis gulosus

DESCRIPTION: More bass-like in form than other pan-fish. Color is overall dark brown, almost black at times, with scattered light markings on sides and fins. Mouth is very large and the jaw extends to the rear of the eye or beyond.

SIZE: Average is 6-8 ounces; few reach one pound; 2-pounders very rare. World record 2 pounds, 7 ounces; Florida record 2.44 pounds.

FOOD VALUE: Excellent.

GAME QUALITIES: Very aggressive striker; good battler for its size.

TACKLE AND BAITS: The works—canepoles, light and ultralight spinning outfits, and fly rods. There's not much a Warmouth won't swallow in the way of a natural bait, but minnows and earthworms are favorites. Nearly the same goes for artificial lures, with the most productive (because of size) being flyrod poppers and streamers, in-line spinners, artificial worms and small surface plugs.

FISHING SYSTEMS: Still Fishing; Casting.

OTHER NAMES:
Warmouth Perch
Black Sunfish
Red-eye

RANGE: *Statewide.*

HABITAT: *Found mostly in very calm water, such as bayous, ditches and sloughs, often in water too muddy for other popular panfish. In large lakes and rivers, their numbers are fewer and they stay close to large snags or undercut banks.*

Bluegill
Lepomis macrochirus

OTHER NAMES:
Bream
Blue Bream
Blue Sunfish
Copperhead

RANGE: *Statewide.*

HABITAT: *Equally at home in lakes, streams and canals. Not so choosy about surroundings as some of the other bream.*

DESCRIPTION: Despite a huge variation in color, the Bluegill is not difficult to identify. It has a rounder shape than other Bream, and a gill flap of solid black with no colored margin. Small individuals are often silvery with a bluish sheen, but the color darkens with growth. Adult females are predominately bluish with light patches. Adult males are purplish, with rust-colored fins and an iridescent patch of coppery scales on the head. Vertical bars of varying shade may be visible at any age.

SIZE: Commonly caught in all sizes, from a couple of ounces to half a pound. Specimens running 8-12 ounces are very common at times, especially when bedding, and fish exceeding 1 pound are not rare. Potential is 3-4 pounds. World record 4 pounds, 12 ounces; Florida record 2.95 pounds.

FOOD VALUE: Variable. Smaller ones are very good; so are big ones, if filleted and skinned rather than scaled.

GAME QUALITIES: Ranks among the best of its size.

TACKLE AND BAITS: Although the most, by far, are caught with poles and any number of natural baits, such as earthworms, crickets and grass shrimp, the Bluegill can stake undisputed claim to the title of Florida's best freshwater flyrod fish. Small poppers and spiders, along with small sinking bugs of any sort are seldom refused when Bluegills are active, and especially deadly during bedding times. Ultralight spinning with tiny spinnerbaits, either cast or trolled, is another effective approach.

FISHING SYSTEMS: Still Fishing; Drifting; Casting; Trolling.

Painted Bream

Lepomis sp.

DESCRIPTION: This colorful fellow is not a separate species, as you might assume from its appearance, but a genetic strain of the Bluegill. Typically, it has a rosy or yellow belly, a coppery dorsal surface, and silvery sides that are marked with irregular black blotches. In some large males, the topside is bright red, rather than copper-colored. It seems thicker, proportionately, than other Bluegills, but has the same solid black gill flap.

SIZE: Like other Bluegills, it's caught in all sizes, including tiny, but is common at 8 ounces or so and runs frequently to 12 ounces. Specimens exceeding a pound are not too unusual.

FOOD VALUE: Excellent.

GAME QUALITIES: One of the scrappiest panfish.

TACKLE AND BAITS: Poles or light spinning outfits get the call, and caterpillars, especially the black-haired pecan worm, are the preferred baits, crickets being runners-up. One of its names, Pecan Bream, derives from its affinity for the pecan worms, which live on— and fall off of—the many pecan trees that border some of the streams in its domain. When pecan worms are in season in late summer, fly casters can take Painted Bream on black, Woolly Worm flies. They will also hit small spinners.

FISHING SYSTEMS: Still Fishing; Drifting; Casting.

OTHER NAMES:
Apalachicola
   Bream
Hand-Painted
   Bream
Pecan Bream

RANGE: *Restricted to the Apalachicola River watershed in the Panhandle, including St. Vincent Island and—due to intermittent flooding—some lakes and ponds in the area. Especially numerous in the Chipola River and Dead Lakes.*

HABITAT: *Most are caught near the shoreline, under overhanging trees along where currents meet eddying water.*

Redear Sunfish "Shellcracker"

Lepomis microlophus

OTHER NAMES:
Yellow Bream

RANGE: *Statewide.*

HABITAT: *Likes soft bottom that's well supplied with its pet foods—the snails and mussels that it cracks to earn its name. Also hangs around grass patches, pads, reeds and snags. In rivers, sticks mostly to slow, deep runs.*

DESCRIPTION: Easily identified by the red spot on the end of its gill flap, the Shellcracker is also less round in shape than other popular bream species. Usual coloration is olive or bluish on the sides, with a bright yellow belly. Variable dark markings—often vertical bars—may also be seen on the sides.

SIZE: This is Florida's largest Bream, reaching weights in excess of four pounds in a few waters. Many 1-pounders are caught all over Florida, and the average during bedding season is often close to 12 ounces. World record 5 pounds, 7 ounces; Florida record 4.86 pounds.

FOOD VALUE: Excellent; tasty fillets that are thicker than those of other Bream.

GAME QUALITIES: Big ones are the toughest panfish.

TACKLE AND BAITS: Poles and earthworms make up the killer combination for Shellcrackers during the spring and summer bedding seasons, when nearly all fishing for them takes place. Many are caught when off the beds, but are difficult to target then, and usually turn up in mixed bags with other panfish. Few fishermen bother to crack out mussels, so the baits used include crickets and grass shrimp, in addition to earthworms. In the way of artificials, they like nearly anything that spins and shines. Although popping bugs account for scattered catches, flyrod fishermen do better with sinking flies—and especially well if a tiny spinner is incorporated into the rig.

FISHING SYSTEMS: Still Fishing; Drifting; Casting.

Redbreast Sunfish
Lepomis auritus

DESCRIPTION: Olive to yellowish on the sides, with bright red male or yellow female belly.

SIZE: Averages 4-6 ounces. World record 1 pound, 12 ounces; Florida record 2.08 pounds.

FOOD VALUE: Best of all the Bream.

GAME QUALITIES: Also tops. Aggressive striker and strong battler for its size.

TACKLE AND BAITS: Canepoles have the widest following, but light spinning tackle is probably even more productive. Fly rods are also excellent. Crickets are the best bait, but worms and caterpillars are fine, too. Spinners and surface plugs are leading artificials.

FISHING SYSTEMS: Drifting; Still Fishing; Casting.

OTHER NAMES:
Redbelly
River Bream
Robin Perch
Yellowbelly

RANGE: Statewide, but uncommon from Lake Okeechobee southward.

HABITAT: A fish of rivers and creeks, where it generally seeks out the swiftest water. Seldom found in lakes except those fed by large streams.

Longear Sunfish
Lepomis megalotis

DESCRIPTION: Sides are brassy with patches and streaks of blue. Belly is bright yellow to orange. The gill flap is long and black but, unlike that of the Redbreast, is edged with white or red.

SIZE: Smaller than the Redbreast; up to 8 or 9 inches. World record 1 pound, 12 ounces.

FOOD VALUE: Excellent.

GAME QUALITIES: Aggressive striker and strong battler for its size.

TACKLE AND BAITS: See Redbreast.

FISHING SYSTEMS: Drifting; Still Fishing; Casting.

OTHER NAMES:
Bigear
Black Tail Sunfish
Redbellied
Bream

RANGE: Found only in the western Panhandle.

HABITAT: Like the Redbreast it inhabits flowing streams, preferring the upper reaches where water is swifter and clear.

Spotted Sunfish "Stumpknocker"

Lepomis punctatus

OTHER NAMES:
Spotted Bream

RANGE: *Statewide.*

HABITAT: *Likes still water, where it waits in ambush under roots and ledges and around stumps and snags.*

DESCRIPTION: Sides are dark, with belly usually cream-colored or light red. Peppered with small black spots.

SIZE: Few Stumpknockers approach a pound in weight. Florida record 0.83 pounds.

FOOD VALUE: Very good, but a great many are too small to bother with.

GAME QUALITIES: Very pugnacious and tough; possibly the most aggressive of all the Bream species, they often hit large artificial lures intended for bass.

TACKLE AND BAITS: Poles work best, and the Stumpknocker will bite an earthworm as quickly as the more expensive or hard-to-find Bream baits. Also quick to hit any of the popular artificial bream baits, such as tiny spinners, jigs, popping bugs and small sinking flies.

FISHING SYSTEMS: Still Fishing; Drifting; Casting.

Flier
Centrarchus macropterus

DESCRIPTION: Black or gray on top, white on lower sides and belly. Liberally sprinkled with black spots. Superficially resembles the Speckled Perch (Black Crappie), except for its small mouth.

SIZE: Seldom more than 6 inches. World record 1 pound, 4 ounces; Florida record 1.24 pounds.

FOOD VALUE: Good, but small and bony.

GAME QUALITIES: Small size makes them easy to haul out of the water on virtually any kind of Bream-fishing tackle.

TACKLE AND BAITS: Fliers are never targeted, except perhaps by children, and so pole and worms are the usual combination. They will, however, take any sort of insect bait, as well as bread balls and kernels of corn; also very small flies and other artificial lures.

FISHING SYSTEMS: Still Fishing; Casting.

OTHER NAMES:
Chinquapin
Bream

RANGE: Probably statewide, but most are caught in North Florida.

HABITAT: Swamp ponds, sloughs and other backwaters. Fliers often share habitat with the Warmouth, which is another species that prefers still water and isn't as particular about the quality of that water as other Bream types would be.

Historically, native populations of Striped Bass have flourished in rivers of the Panhandle and Northeast Florida, but scientists are now struggling to maintain the viability of both stocks. Pretty good fisheries remain in those areas, thanks to regular stocking of hatchery fish. The White Bass, found only in a limited area of the Panhandle, is a smaller relative that lacks the size of the Striper but none of its aggressiveness. Put those two together and you get the Sunshine Bass, a hybrid known to anglers all over the state, thanks to regular stocking in many lakes and streams by the Florida Game and Fresh Water Fish Commission. The name "Sunshine Bass" is strictly Floridian, having been determined by means of a public contest.

Basses With Stripes

Striped Bass
White Bass
Sunshine Bass

Striped Bass

Morone saxatilis

OTHER NAMES:

Striper

Rock Bass

RANGE: *The St. Marys and St. Johns Rivers of the Northeast Florida coast, and also the Panhandle from Pensacola Bay to the Ochlockonee River.*

HABITAT: *In the Panhandle, Stripers are caught from lakes Woodruff and Talquin and from bays—especially Pensacola, Choctawhatchee and West Bays. The most famous West Florida spot is the swift water below the Woodruff Dam on the Apalachicola at Chattahoochee. A similar but smaller fishery exists at the Talquin Dam on SR 20 west of Tallahassee. In the rivers below the dams—as in the Northeast Florida rivers— anglers generally search for their stripers where deep, running water abuts shallow points, eddies, bars and runoffs.*

DESCRIPTION: Heavy-bodied with long head and underslung jaw. Color is usually dark green to dark gray above, silvery on the sides and belly. There are 7 or 8 longitudinal stripes that are generally regular and unbroken.

SIZE: Can reach 50 pounds or more, but most run 5-20. World record 78 pounds, 8 ounces; Florida record 43 pounds, 9 ounces.

FOOD VALUE: Very good; light, rich flesh.

GAME QUALITIES: Stubborn and strong; a tough challenge for the angler, particularly in strong current.

TACKLE AND BAITS: Below the dams, heavy spinning tackle and light to medium ocean outfits or surf outfits are preferred. Baitfish—mostly small Shad—are usually scooped up on the spot with long-handled nets. Artificial lures are productive below the dams at times, and are the first choices in bays and lakes where many Stripers are sight-fished when they school on top. Some of the best lures are weighted spoons, shad-type underwater swimmers and floating-diving plugs of various makes; also jigs with trailers of pork rind or plastic worm. The same baits are prominent in the St. Marys and St. Johns, where both casting and trolling are practiced by Striper fans, most of whom fish with medium spinning rigs or baitcasting tackle.

FISHING SYSTEMS: Casting; Trolling; Still Fishing.

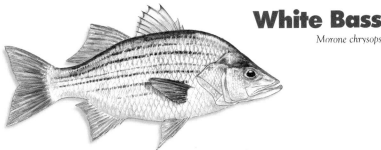

White Bass
Morone chrysops

DESCRIPTION: A glance discloses the White's relationship to the Striper. The coloration and stripes are dead giveaways.

SIZE: Usually 1 to 2 pounds. World record 6 pounds, 13 ounces; Florida record 4.69 pounds.

FOOD VALUE: Good.

GAME QUALITIES: Aggressive striker and hard fighter on light tackle.

TACKLE AND BAITS: Light spinning and baitcasting gear. Best lures include spoons, jigs and small topwater or floating-diving plugs. Live minnows also work—deep-drifted in lakes, or fished around points.

FISHING SYSTEMS: Casting; Drifting; Still Fishing.

OTHER NAMES:
Silver Bass

RANGE: *Found only in the Panhandle, mostly in lakes Woodruff and Talquin, and their adjacent streams.*

HABITAT: *Most White Bass are caught when schools of them romp to the surface to feed on schools of baitfish. This usually happens early and late in the day, although "jumps" can occur throughout the day in cool weather.*

Sunshine Bass
Morone saxatilis x chrysops

DESCRIPTION: Almost a dead ringer for a Striped Bass, but is easily distinguished by the stripes on the lower side, which are broken and irregular.

SIZE: Reaches 8 or 10 pounds. Florida record 16.31 pounds.

FOOD VALUE: Very good.

GAME QUALITIES: Outstanding; not easy to fool, and a terrific battler.

TACKLE AND BAITS: Light spinning and baitcasting tackle. Best naturals are small Shad and store-bought Shiners. Small, shad-like crankbaits are good lures in lakes. River fishermen tend to fish live Shiners.

FISHING SYSTEMS: Still Fishing; Trolling; Casting.

OTHER NAMES:
Hybrid
Whiterock Bass

RANGE: *No natural range, but regularly stocked in many lakes and streams all over Florida.*

HABITAT: *Like its two parents, the Sunshine Bass likes to stay deep most of the time, surfacing to chase bait at times. It is particularly fond of deep holes around bends.*

Unglamorous they may be, but Catfish have few peers on the dinner table and they provide a great deal of fun for a great many fishermen, some of whom enjoy using bushlines and trotlines as much as most anglers enjoy poles and rods. Bushlines are simply heavy lines, baited and tied before dark to springy bushes overhanging a river. They are checked several times during the night and any catches collected. The typical bushline outing ends with a fish fry on the riverbank.

Freshwater catfish have dorsal and pectoral spines that are as hard and sharp as those of their saltwater cousins, so the angler has to take care in handling them. However, a puncture from a freshwater cat, although no laughing matter, is not likely to be so serious or painful.

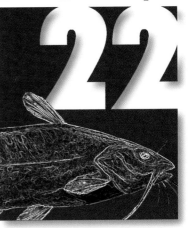

The Catfishes

Flathead Catfish

Pylodictis olivaris

RANGE: *Escambia, Apalachicola and Ochlockonee Rivers of the Panhandle. May be spreading.*

HABITAT: *Sticks to deep holes and undercuts during the day; forages widely at night.*

DESCRIPTION: Overall brown with shadings of gold or yellow. White tip on upper lobe of tail, head is wide and flat; tail is square.

SIZE: The largest Florida catfish, it can grow to 100 pounds, but the usual maximum is around 50. Catches commonly cover all size ranges from a couple of pounds to 20 or more. World record 123 pounds, 9 ounces; Florida record 48.3 pounds.

FOOD VALUE: Very good.

GAME QUALITIES: Not spectacular, but has the size and strength to give an angler a rough workout.

TACKLE AND BAITS: Poles and light tackle are fine for potluck fishing, but if targeting the big ones, use heavy spinning or baitcasting tackle with lines up to 20-pound test—or even light saltwater gear. Best baits for trophy-size Flatheads are live or fresh-dead Bream, Shad and other fairly small fish. Like all Catfish, Flatheads of average size go for a great variety of baits that includes not only insects, worms and aquatic life, but also homemade offerings such as cheese, liver and various smelly concoctions.

FISHING SYSTEMS: Still Fishing.

Channel Catfish

Ictalurus punctatus

DESCRIPTION: Light blue or gray on top, silvery below, with many black spots. The tail is forked. Big fish often are almost black.

SIZE: Anywhere from 4 or 5 inches to 40 or 50 pounds. World record 58 pounds; Florida record 44.50 pounds.

FOOD VALUE: Excellent. Small ones from 6 to about 12 inches are considered the best-eating of Catfish.

GAME QUALITIES: Big specimens pull hard and long.

TACKLE AND BAITS: "Eating size" fish in the rivers are good targets for light spinning tackle and small baits, such as earthworms, crickets and cut baits. For a trophy catch, try heavier gear—and live Shiners or Bream.

FISHING SYSTEMS: Still Fishing.

OTHER NAMES:
Forktail
Speckled Cat
Silver Cat
River Cat

RANGE: *Statewide, due to transplanting.*

HABITAT: *Fishing is best in flowing streams, concentrating on deep holes during the day. In canals and lakes, try areas where creeks or other flowing water comes in.*

White Catfish

Ameiurus catus

DESCRIPTION: Similar to small Channel Cat, but lighter and without spots. Tail slightly forked.

SIZE: Averages ½ to 1 pound; seldom more than 2. Florida and world records 19 pounds, 5 ounces.

FOOD VALUE: Excellent.

GAME QUALITIES: Tugs fairly hard, but no challenge.

TACKLE AND BAITS: Pole or light spinning outfit, with worms or crickets as bait; probably takes most of them, but they will bite nearly any natural bait.

FISHING SYSTEMS: Still Fishing.

RANGE: *Most of Florida; rare or absent south of Lake Okeechobee.*

HABITAT: *Much the same as the Channel Cat.*

Yellow Bullhead

Ameiurus natalis

OTHER NAMES:
Yellow Cat
Butter Cat
Mudcat

RANGE: Statewide.

HABITAT: Lakes, ponds and slow streams; soft bottom.

DESCRIPTION: Brown on top, yellowish below. Square tail. Chin barbels are white.

SIZE: Usually under 1 pound; rarely 2 pounds. World record 4 pounds, 15 ounces.

FOOD VALUE: Very good.

GAME QUALITIES: Fun but no challenge.

TACKLE AND BAITS: Pole or light spinning outfit; worms and other small natural baits—or cheese, or cut bait—fished on bottom.

FISHING SYSTEMS: Still Fishing.

Brown Bullhead

Ameiurus nebulosus

OTHER NAMES:
Brown Catfish
Black Catfish
Butter Cat

RANGE: Statewide.

HABITAT: Lakes, ponds and slow streams; soft bottom.

DESCRIPTION: Brown above, cream or yellow on sides, with brown mottling. Square tail.

SIZE: Usually under 1 pound; rarely 2 pounds. World record 6 pounds, 5 ounces. Florida record 5 pounds, 11 ounces.

FOOD VALUE: Very good.

GAME QUALITIES: Fun but no challenge.

TACKLE AND BAITS: Pole or light spinning outfit; worms and other small natural baits—or cheese, or cut bait.

FISHING SYSTEMS: Still Fishing.

Spotted Bullhead

Ameiurus serracanthus

DESCRIPTION: Dark brown or gray above, brownish on sides, with numerous white spots.

SIZE: Under 1 pound.

FOOD VALUE: Excellent.

GAME QUALITIES: Pulls fairly hard, but lacks size.

TACKLE AND BAITS: Pole or light spinning outfit, with worms or crickets as bait, takes most of them.

FISHING SYSTEMS: Still Fishing.

OTHER NAMES:
Speckled Cat

RANGE: *Restricted to a few watersheds in North Florida, from the Suwannee west to the Apalachicola.*

HABITAT: *Likes brisk currents and is most common in smaller tributaries, rather than the principal rivers in its range.*

Walking Catfish

Clarias batrachus

DESCRIPTION: An invader from Asia that has little similarity to native Catfishes, it has a long, dark gray body with rounded tail. Mouth is flat with eight barbels. Pectoral fins are curved downward and serve as "feet" when the fish travels on land—as it can do, thanks to a supplementary air-breathing organ.

SIZE: Usually 10-12 inches; may reach 2 feet. World record 2 pounds, 10 ounces.

FOOD VALUE: Scrawny and seldom eaten.

GAME QUALITIES: None.

TACKLE AND BAITS: Not targeted.

FISHING SYSTEMS: Still Fishing.

RANGE: *Widely established in South Florida, and sometimes encountered in other areas of the state. Cold weather apparently has kept it fairly well limited in both range and population—much to the relief of environmentalists.*

HABITAT: *Mostly in South Florida canals, but it can live in virtually any watery habitat. Its walking, or migrating, takes place on wet nights.*

Shad are counted among the Herrings—a large family of fishes whose diets generally preclude them as targets of hook-and-line fishermen. However, the American Shad, Alabama Shad and Hickory Shad are among the few Herrings that are both large enough and predacious enough to develop an angling following. In Florida, this following is almost entirely devoted to runs of the American Shad in the St. Johns River. Catches of Hickory Shad, also in the St. Johns, and of Alabama Shad in rivers of the Panhandle may not be much less enjoyable but are not nearly so common. Two other Shad—the Gizzard and Threadfin—are much smaller and their role in the world of Florida angling is to serve as forage, chum and bait.

23

The Shads

American Shad

Hickory Shad

Alabama Shad

Gizzard Shad

American Shad

Alosa sapidissima

RANGE: The St. Marys and St. Johns Rivers of Northeast Florida.

HABITAT: Shad live at sea but run upriver to spawn, beginning about mid-January. That's when anglers find them in mostly well-known spots or areas in the river, most of them near DeLand and Sanford in Central Florida.

DESCRIPTION: Gray to greenish above, with silvery sides. The fins are soft. A dark spot just aft of the gill cover is followed by a series of smaller black dots.

SIZE: Average catch runs 1-4 pounds. World record 11 pounds, 4 ounces; Florida record 5.19 pounds.

FOOD VALUE: Very good, but very bony. Excellent smoked. Roe is a famous delicacy.

GAME QUALITIES: A terrific and showy battler, nick-named by many "freshwater Tarpon."

TACKLE AND BAITS: The majority of Shad are caught with spinning or baitcasting tackle and silver spoons or jigs. Most fish hit near bottom.

FISHING SYSTEMS: Trolling; Casting.

Hickory Shad

Alosa mediocris

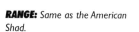

RANGE: Same as the American Shad.

HABITAT: Also a sea dweller that spawns in the rivers. Usually seeks out branches of creeks, although some mix with American Shad in the big water.

DESCRIPTION: Looks like the American Shad, but is generally smaller and often darker. Unlike the American Shad, lower jaw is longer than the upper.

SIZE: Averages around 1 pound; some hit 2 or 3 pounds. World record 2 pounds, 8 ounces.

FOOD VALUE: Good but bony.

GAME QUALITIES: Outstanding for its size.

TACKLE AND BAITS: Same as for American Shad. Most catches are incidental to fishing for Bass or Speckled Perch, with small lures and minnows.

FISHING SYSTEMS: Trolling; Casting; Drifting.

Alabama Shad

Alosa alabamae

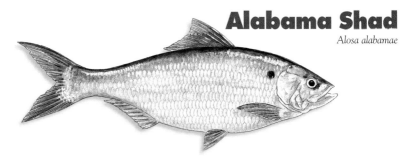

DESCRIPTION: Similar to the species already covered, but easy to differentiate by geography alone, and by the fact that it has only a single spot behind the gill.

SIZE: Usually around a pound or slightly less; sometimes 2 pounds.

FOOD VALUE: Good but bony.

GAME QUALITIES: Fine fighter, but seldom gets to show it off.

TACKLE AND BAITS: Will hit small jigs, spoons and flies, and light spinning or fly tackle would be the most sporting.

FISHING SYSTEMS: Could try trolling or deep casting in open water.

RANGE: Larger rivers of the Panhandle, from the Suwannee westward.

HABITAT: Spawning runs take place from late winter to summer. Likes deep, mid-river water.

Gizzard Shad

Dorosoma cepedianum

DESCRIPTION: The Gizzard Shad, shown here, and the **Threadfin Shad**, *Dorosoma petenense*, are virtually dead ringers. The Gizzard Shad has spots inside and out of the mouth. Both kinds have the long, threadlike trailer off the dorsal fin. World record 4 pounds, 6 ounces.

SIZE: Most run 2-6 inches long.

FOOD VALUE: Not eaten.

GAME QUALITIES: None.

TACKLE AND BAITS: None productive.

FISHING SYSTEMS: Cast netting.

RANGE: Larger rivers and many lakes throughout Florida.

HABITAT: Open water.

Cichlids comprise a huge family of fishes native to South America, Asia and Africa. So why are there so many of them in Florida? By accident and stupidity, for the most part, although one type was deliberately introduced by fishery managers to provide a major new freshwater gamefish. That one, of course, was the Peacock Bass. All the smaller Cichlids have become established in Florida after escaping—or being liberated—from private aquariums.

Most are restricted by climate to Southeast Florida below Lake Okeechobee, but some have taken up residence in other parts of the state. Out of at least a dozen Cichlid species now thriving in Florida, only two—the Peacock Bass and the Oscar—have proven to be attractive and cooperative additions to Florida's gamefish menu.

Another, the Jaguar Guapote, seems ready to join them as a legitimate sporting target, and the Black Acara is caught fairly often by canepole fishermen seeking Bream or Oscars.

24

The Cichlids

Peacock Cichlid

Oscar

Jaguar Guapote

Black Acara

Midas Cichlid

Mayan Cichlid

Blue Tilapia

Peacock Cichlid "Peacock Bass"

Cichla ocellaris

OTHER NAMES:

Butterfly Bass
Butterfly Cichlid
Butterfly Peacock

RANGE: *A warm-water species restricted to deep canals and their adjacent lakes in the Miami-Fort Lauderdale area (Dade and Broward Counties). Those waters have depths where the temperature never falls below the Peacock's tolerance level, even during the occasional freeze. The species may creep northward during protracted warm periods, but outside Dade and Broward it is subject to being killed back during a harsh winter.*

HABITAT: *Like the Largemouth Bass that share its waters, Peacocks usually stick close to grass or other structure.*

DESCRIPTION: Bass-like shape and large mouth with underslung jaw. Very colorful—green to black dorsal surface with yellow or cream-colored sides, marked by vertical black bars, and one huge black spot with a white margin—the "peacock eye"—on the upper lobe of the caudal fin. Large males also have a red stripe on side and a pronounced hump forward of the dorsal fin. A similar and larger species, the **Speckled Peacock, *Cichla temensis***, was introduced along with this one, but did not adapt and is now rarely seen.

SIZE: Averages 1-2 pounds; lunkers run 3-5 pounds; maximum is perhaps 8 or 9 pounds. World record 12 pounds, 9 ounces; Florida record 9.08 pounds.

FOOD VALUE: Very good.

GAME QUALITIES: Hard striker and strong, acrobatic fighter. Most anglers consider it tougher than a Largemouth of equal size. As an added bonus for sleep-in anglers, Peacocks do not like to bite early in the morning—or at night.

TACKLE AND BAITS: Rather light spinning and bait-casting tackle with lines testing up to 12 or 15 pounds. Live shiners are almost a can't-miss bait, but many anglers prefer to cast with lures. Among the best offerings are topwater plugs, crankbaits and spoons, worked steadily and fairly fast. Skip plastic worms; Peacock Bass don't like them at all. For flies, try large streamers—marabou seems particularly appealing—and strip them quickly.

FISHING SYSTEMS: Casting; Still Fishing; Trolling.

Oscar

Astronotus ocellatus

DESCRIPTION: Very thick, compressed body. Color is overall dark brown, but often with lighter mottling that can take the form of orange bars. There is always an ocellus or red-ringed spot on the tail, and usually one or two others on the posterior dorsal fin. Caudal, dorsal and anal fins are rounded and fanlike— reminiscent of the saltwater Tripletail.

SIZE: Averages perhaps a half-pound; sometimes tops 1 pound but seldom reaches 2. Florida and world records 3 pounds, 8 ounces.

FOOD VALUE: Very good. Even the average fish is thick enough to provide nice little fillets.

GAME QUALITIES: Strong for a panfish.

TACKLE AND BAITS: Canepoles and worms often produce long stringers, but Oscars are aggressive and usually hungry and will hit both plastic worms and "hard" casting lures, including small topwater plugs and spinners. Fly rodders can catch them on popping bugs or 1-2-inch streamer flies.

FISHING SYSTEMS: Casting; Still Fishing.

OTHER NAMES:
Velvet Cichlid

RANGE: *Originally introduced in southern Dade County (Miami area) in the late 1950s, the Oscar has since spread to most of the inland waters south of Lake Okeechobee—from East Coast to West. It is present in canals around the big lake and will probably expand even farther north.*

HABITAT: *Likes still or sluggish water with weeds.*

Jaguar Guapote

Cichlasoma managuense

DESCRIPTION: Thick-bodied and somewhat similar to the Oscar in shape, but the dorsal and anal fins are pointed. The color is quite different, olive on the back, shading to gold with a purple sheen on the sides. Many small purple spots also dot the sides, which may be marked with a row of black squares as well. The mouth is very large.

SIZE: Runs to at least 2 pounds. The author has caught a number of three-pounders in Nicaragua. World and Florida record 3 pound, 8 ounces.

FOOD VALUE: Very tasty.

GAME QUALITIES: Aggressive striker and an excellent fighter for its size.

TACKLE AND BAITS: Light spinning, baitcasting or fly outfits. Hits a variety of artificials, headed by small spinners and surface plugs. Also takes popping bugs and streamer flies. Minnows and small shiners are the leading natural baits.

FISHING SYSTEMS: Still Fishing; Casting.

Black Acara

Cichlasoma bimaculatum

DESCRIPTION: Similar to the Oscar in shape, but color is much lighter, being predominately gray or whitish with dark spots on the side that link to form a jagged stripe. The caudal fin is round, as with the Oscar, but the dorsal and anal fins are pointed.

SIZE: Averages a half-pound or less; may hit 1 pound.

FOOD VALUE: Good.

GAME QUALITIES: A spunky panfish, but neither as pugnacious nor as strong a fighter as the Oscar, which inhabits many of the same waters.

TACKLE AND BAITS: Most are caught by canepolers using worms or minnows. Seldom takes artificial lures, although a few are caught on tiny spinners and on sinking flies.

FISHING SYSTEMS: Still Fishing.

RANGE: *Canals of Southeast Florida, north to at least Palm Beach County and the canals around Lake Okeechobee.*

HABITAT: *Prefers grassy areas with soft bottom, but is widely distributed throughout a variety of canal surroundings.*

Midas Cichlid

Cichlasoma citrinellum

OTHER NAMES:
Golden Cichlid

RANGE: *South Dade County.*

HABITAT: *Mostly residential canals.*

DESCRIPTION: Large males are usually golden with bars and other dark markings, but coloration is highly variable. Many are dull gray or white with black markings.

SIZE: Less than a pound.

FOOD VALUE: Good.

GAME QUALITIES: Minimal.

TACKLE AND BAITS: Commonly spotted in the water by anglers because of their bright color, but not often caught. Will bite worms or, at times, very small artificial lures.

FISHING SYSTEMS: Still Fishing; Casting.

Mayan Cichlid

Cichlasoma urophthalmus

OTHER NAMES:
Pez Maya

RANGE: *South Dade County; Everglades National Park.*

HABITAT: *Some in canals, but anglers see most of them in brackish, or even salty, backwaters of the National Park. Probably the only Cichlid in Florida with a tolerance for salt water.*

DESCRIPTION: Yellow or gold with dark vertical bars on the side, reminiscent of the saltwater Sheepshead. Red throat and belly. Pointed dorsal and anal fins.

SIZE: A good-size Cichlid, averaging perhaps $1/2$ pound and capable of exceeding 1 pound. World and Florida records, 2 pounds, 8 ounces.

FOOD VALUE: Very good, but should be skinned.

GAME QUALITIES: A spunky panfish.

TACKLE AND BAITS: Light spinning and baitcasting rigs with small jigs, spoons, spinners or live shrimp.

FISHING SYSTEMS: Casting; Still Fishing.

Blue Tilapia

Tilapia aurea

DESCRIPTION: Powdery blue from back to lower sides and white below; marked by three or four vertical bars and numerous small black spots.

SIZE: Common at 2-4 pounds. World and Florida records, 9 pounds.

FOOD VALUE: Very good, but seldom available as a sporting catch. Widely caught and sold commercially.

GAME QUALITIES: A good fighter, although rarely hooked. This fish was mistakenly introduced in place of the Nile Tilapia, which is a small game species that strikes a variety of baits and lures. The Blue Tilapia, however, hits almost nothing that an angler uses for bait.

TACKLE AND BAITS: Eats algae and minute insect life and so is caught only rarely and accidentally on a baited line. Good target for bow fishing, which is legal in many waters (check local laws).

FISHING SYSTEMS: Cast netting; Bow fishing; rarely Still Fishing.

OTHER NAMES:
Nile Perch

RANGE: Widespread and too plentiful in many lakes throughout the Florida Peninsula, having expanded widely since being brought into Central Florida in 1961, in the mistaken belief that it would control grass.

HABITAT: Soft bottom; often in shoreline shallows.

Gars are primitive fishes—and they look it, with their armor-like scales and long bills with many sharp teeth. Whether they fish for them or not, or get harassed by them or not, anglers can't help being familiar with Gars because they are present in nearly all waters and are highly visible, due to their habit of rolling at the surface in order to gulp air. Their anatomy includes a sort of rudimentary lung that helps out their gills. One of them, the Alligator Gar, is the largest predatory freshwater fish in North America.

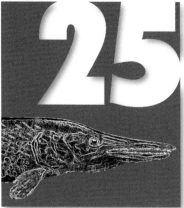

The Gars

Alligator Gar
Longnose Gar
Florida Gar

Alligator Gar

Lepisosteus spatula

OTHER NAMES:
Great Gar
Manjuari

RANGE: *Western Panhandle, mainly the Apalachicola and Escambia Rivers, but present to some extent near the mouths of smaller rivers, such as the Ochlockonee.*

HABITAT: *Free-roaming, but usually seen in the middle reaches of the rivers. Also ventures into salt water and sometimes startles anglers who are drifting over shallow grass beds when it rolls near their boat.*

DESCRIPTION: Usually identifiable by size alone, and by the short, very wide snout. If still in doubt (and brave enough) check the teeth—the Alligator Gar has two rows on each side of the mouth, top and bottom, while other Gars have only one. Color usually is dark brown above, yellow below, with a thin strip from head to tail. Few, if any, spots on most individuals.

SIZE: Grows to 10 feet long and more than 300 pounds, but the great majority weigh less than 100 pounds. Average is probably 25-75 pounds. World record 279 pounds; Florida record 123 pounds.

FOOD VALUE: Seldom eaten. Flesh would be okay, but roe is often toxic.

GAME QUALITIES: A roughhouse battler and a challenge to land because of sheer size, but not very swift.

TACKLE AND BAITS : One hits a big plug or other artificial lure now and then, but anglers who fish for Alligator Gar use very heavy spinning tackle or saltwater gear, and bait with live fish suspended near the surface with a float.

FISHING SYSTEMS: Still Fishing; Drifting.

Longnose Gar

Lepisosteus osseus

DESCRIPTION: Brown or dark green on top and sides; creamy or white underneath.

SIZE: The largest Gar found in most of Florida, it can grow to perhaps 6 feet. Average size is in the 5-15-pound range. World record 50 pounds, 5 ounces; Florida record 41 pounds.

FOOD VALUE: Very good, but unpopular and difficult to clean. Roe is often poisonous.

GAME QUALITIES: Size makes it fun, but the fight wouldn't stand up against many saltwater fish.

TACKLE AND BAITS: Baitcasting or heavy spinning gear, with line up to 20-pound test. Best baits are live Shiners or Bream, fished near the surface. The hard beak makes them next to impossible to hook. Small, sharp treble hooks help.

FISHING SYSTEMS: Still Fishing.

OTHER NAMES:
Garfish
Longnose

RANGE: *All of North Florida and also peninsular Florida to about the Kissimmee Chain of Lakes. A few individuals wander into Lake Okeechobee, or even farther south on rare occasion.*

HABITAT: *Open water.*

Florida Gar

Lepisosteus platyrhincus

DESCRIPTION: The Florda Gar, shown here, and the **Spotted Gar**, *Lepisosteus oculatus*, are virtually identical, but have separate ranges. Both are brown above, lighter below, and wear many brown and black spots.

SIZE: Average for both is 2-4 pounds. World and Florida record 10 pounds.

FOOD VALUE: Not at all popular but very good, and a traditional favorite of South Florida Indians. Remember, though: Gar roe can be toxic.

GAME QUALITIES: Next to none.

TACKLE AND BAITS: Will strike—or at least worry— various artificial lures, mainly spoons, spinners and surface plugs. They delight, too, in ruining live shiners being fished for Bass.

FISHING SYSTEMS: Still Fishing; Casting.

RANGE: *The* **Spotted Gar** *is found only in a small corner of Florida, from the Apalachicola River west to the Alabama line. The* **Florida Gar** *is plentiful everywhere else in the state.*

HABITAT: *Free roaming, but they much prefer still or stagnant waters of canals, ponds and lakes, or slow bends and backwaters of streams.*

The Chain Pickerel is a fine gamefish, but unappreciated. The Sturgeon is endangered in Florida, and fishermen sometimes wish that the Mudfish were too. The Golden Shiner is a favorite bait, and the Eel is a frightful catch—at least for a few of the more timid souls. The Bigmouth is even scarier-looking than the Eel but just as harmless. Carp are strong pullers but don't end up on many fishing lines in Florida. Put these all together and you have the final section of this book.

Miscellaneous Freshwater Species

Chain Pickerel

Redfin Pickerel

Golden Shiner

Grass Carp

Common Carp

Atlantic Sturgeon

Bigmouth Sleeper

American Eel

Bowfin

Chain Pickerel

Esox niger

OTHER NAMES:
Jackfish
Freshwater Jack

RANGE: *Statewide.*

HABITAT: *Nearly always found in close association with grass, pads or other vegetation, or around stumps and snags.*

DESCRIPTION: Long, lean and mean-looking, with a long, wide mouth and many small teeth. Coloration is greenish above, brown or yellowish on the sides, with chain-like markings.

SIZE: Averages 1 or 2 pounds; 3-4-pounders earn praise; can grow to around 9 pounds. World record 9 pounds, 6 ounces; Florida record 5.75 pounds.

FOOD VALUE: Pickerel have an excellent flavor but many small bones throughout the flesh turn most fishermen away from them in the dining department. Those who do eat Pickerel often prepare them by filleting (leaving the skin on) and then making numerous slashes all along the length of each fillet, without cutting through the skin. This severs many of the little bones, which subsequently dissolve or soften when the fillets are deep-fried.

GAME QUALITIES: As aggressive as it looks, the Pickerel strikes viciously and is a fine gamester for its size, getting off zippy runs and thrashing jumps.

TACKLE AND BAITS: Baitcasting or spinning outfits with lines up to 12-pound test will give the most sport. Although Pickerel will hit just about any artificial lure intended for bass, shiny spoons and spinners are the best attractors, with surface plugs not far behind. Pickerel love live Shiners—much to the distress of live-bait bass fishermen.

FISHING SYSTEMS: Casting; Still Fishing.

Redfin Pickerel

Esox americanus americanus

DESCRIPTION: Looks like a small Chain Pickerel, but with an overall reddish cast. Fins are also red, as opposed to the dark green or gray of the Chain Pickerel's.

SIZE: Seldom more than 12 inches long. World record 2 pounds, 4 ounces; Florida record 1.06 pounds.

FOOD VALUE: Excellent. Bones are as plentiful as in the Chain Pickerel, but they are softer, due to the Redfin's small size. Dressed fish are usually fried whole and eaten bones and all.

GAME QUALITIES: Like its bigger relatives, the Redfin is always ready to pick a fight, but lacks the heft to put up much of a battle.

TACKLE AND BAITS: Poles, light spinning rods and light fly rods. They're often difficult to fish because of the thick weeds they usually inhabit, so very small weedless lures are needed. As productive as any is a little strip of pork rind, or even red fabric, skittered across the surface on a small weedless hook. Small minnows make the best natural bait.

FISHING SYSTEMS: Casting; Still Fishing.

OTHER NAMES:
Pike

RANGE: Statewide.

HABITAT: Mostly small waters, such as ponds and still creeks or runs, that are shallow and grassy.

Golden Shiner

Notemigonus crysoleucas

OTHER NAMES:
**Roach Shiner
Bitterhead
Shiner**

RANGE: Statewide.

HABITAT: Shiners are found in all sorts of water, from large lakes to roadside ditches. They generally stick close to cover, especially thick grass and lily pads.

DESCRIPTION: Long, thin body with large scales that usually flash gold in color but may be silver in very clear water. Small head with upturned mouth. Forked tail.

SIZE: From a couple of inches to more than 12 inches.

FOOD VALUE: None. Very bony; they are nearly always used for bait, not food.

GAME QUALITIES: Next to none. Shiners are frequently hooked by pole fishermen seeking bream, but they don't put much bend in the pole. They are, however, enjoyable for youngsters to catch and, in many cases, can be found where there are no Bream.

TACKLE AND BAITS: "Wild" Shiners—as opposed to those raised on bait farms—are the most beloved baits of Bass fishermen. Those who don't wish to buy them, or can't find them, can usually catch at least a few by chumming around a grass or lily-pad bed with hooks baited with bits of earthworm or doughballs. They also can be chummed and cast netted, but be sure to check laws relating to possession of cast nets while bass fishing.

FISHING SYSTEMS: Still Fishing.

Grass Carp

Ctenopharyngodon idella

DESCRIPTION: Rather slim body. Dark green to brownish above; yellowish below. Frontal mouth with no barbels. Large scales.

SIZE: Most are 5-15 pounds; potential much larger. World record 80 pounds.

FOOD VALUE: Poor.

GAME QUALITIES: Sluggish fighter.

TACKLE AND BAITS: Spinning or baitcasting tackle with doughballs or other Carp baits.

FISHING SYSTEMS: Still Fishing.

OTHER NAMES:
White Amur

RANGE: Introduced into various Florida lakes and canals as weed control agents.

HABITAT: Shallow, grassy areas with soft bottom.

Common Carp

Cyprinus carpio

DESCRIPTION: Greenish above and whitish below. Often has an overall red or gold cast, with reddish tail. Has two barbels on each side of the small mouth.

SIZE: From a pound to 20 pounds. World record 75 pounds, 11 ounces; Florida record 40.56 pounds.

FOOD VALUE: Not highly regarded. Very bony.

GAME QUALITIES: A surprisingly strong fighter, but no great challenge to the angler.

TACKLE AND BAITS: Rods must be scaled to the size being sought. Baits are usually doughballs, cheeseballs or some other "secret" concoction, but earthworms work pretty well.

FISHING SYSTEMS: Still Fishing.

OTHER NAMES:
European Carp

RANGE: Of Eurasian origin, the Carp has spread widely throughout the U.S. but in Florida is common only in the northern counties. A minor fishery exists in the Apalachicola watershed, and in some private or municipal ponds, where it was once stocked.

HABITAT: Shallow, grassy water with soft bottom.

Atlantic Sturgeon

Acipenser oxyrhynchus

RANGE: *Sturgeon are still probably present in most of the large rivers of North and Central Florida, including the Suwannee, St. Johns, Apalachicola and Escambia, but if you happen to catch one, toss it back. The species is endangered in Florida, after being commercially fished since about the turn of the century.*

HABITAT: *Deep riverbeds over mud, gravel or sand.*

DESCRIPTION: The Sturgeon is a large, prehistoric-looking, armor-plated fish with long, upturned snout. Few anglers ever get to see one in Florida.

SIZE: Among the largest of freshwater fishes, capable of growing to 14 feet and several hundred pounds.

FOOD VALUE: Sturgeons have tasty flesh and some specimens contain caviar, but they're fully protected in Florida.

GAME QUALITIES: Because of sheer size, any hooked Sturgeon would be a tough customer indeed.

TACKLE AND BAITS: Not much of a sport fishery ever developed for Sturgeon in Florida.

FISHING SYSTEMS: Don't try it!

Bigmouth Sleeper

Gobiomorus dormitor

OTHER NAMES:
Guabina
Rock Bass

RANGE: *Large islands of the Caribbean and probably much of Florida, although most reported catches are from Palm Beach, Broward and Dade Counties. Not rare, but seldom caught.*

HABITAT: *Likes rocks or cover.*

DESCRIPTION: Long, cylindrical body with wide head, large mouth and round tail. Color is mottled brown.

SIZE: A pound or so on average; may reach three pounds.

FOOD VALUE: Very good; highly prized in the tropics.

GAME QUALITIES: Not much of a battler.

TACKLE AND BAITS: Usually taken (with great surprise) by anglers casting for Bass or Snook in Southeast Florida.

FISHING SYSTEMS: Casting; Still Fishing.

American Eel

Anguilla rostrata

DESCRIPTION: Snakelike body with pointed head. Small pectoral fins. Dorsal, caudal and anal fins are combined into one long fin. Dark gray to olive above, yellowish or white on underside.

SIZE: About 2 feet on average; sometimes to 3 or 4 feet. World record 9 pounds, 4 ounces.

FOOD VALUE: Prized by some; difficult to clean.

GAME QUALITIES: Not much.

TACKLE AND BAITS: Caught mostly on trotlines, or by bottom-fishing at night with worms or catfish baits.

FISHING SYSTEMS: Still Fishing.

OTHER NAMES:
Common Eel

RANGE: *Most, if not all, coastal streams of Florida, Cuba, Puerto Rico and Jamaica. A few wander far inland to tributaries, and even make it into lakes. The Eel is one of the most widely distributed of all fishes—spawning in a common ground at sea and then returning to coastal waters.*

HABITAT: *Hides during the day under rocks or logs. Forages at night, which is why few are caught by anglers.*

Bowfin "Mudfish"

Amia calva

DESCRIPTION: It has a rudimentary air-breathing capability and gulps air at the surface. Dark brown, sometimes with yellowish patterns on the sides. The mouth is fitted with small, sharp teeth.

SIZE: Averages 2-5 pounds; fairly common to 6 or 8 pounds. World record 21 pounds, 8 ounces; Florida record 19 pounds.

FOOD VALUE: Edible, but not usually eaten.

GAME QUALITIES: Hard striker and a tough, surface-thrashing battler.

TACKLE AND BAITS: Can be caught—like it or not—on any kind of Bass tackle, lures and baits.

FISHING SYSTEMS: Casting; Still Fishing.

OTHER NAMES:
Blackfish
Grindle
Cypress Bass

RANGE: *Statewide.*

HABITAT: *Likes still or sluggish water and can tolerate low oxygen levels. Likes to lurk under or around cypress trunks, stumps, pads or grass beds.*

Index

The Women Anglers of FLORIDA SPORTSMAN 2012 CALENDAR

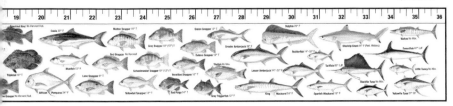

The Fishiest of Authors

If you had to choose one person who knows his Florida fish and how to catch them better than any other angler of our time, it would have to be Vic Dunaway.

Vic's seen virtually all of them, up close, on the end of his fishing line.

Moreover, Vic has sampled the culinary value of seemingly every finny thing that swims.

In this Sport Fish of Florida book, Vic shares with you his half-century of experience, telling you how to I.D. a fish, how to catch it, where it resides and whether it's good to eat. (You may find that you've been discarding some fish that are actually excellent table fare.)

Vic is no snob when it comes to finding good food. We can all benefit from his hard-earned knowledge.

As founding editor of Florida Sportsman Magazine, author of best-selling books, contributor to national magazines, and TV personality, Vic is widely acclaimed as the dean of Florida outdoor writers, an expert who plies quiet streams for bluegill one day and searches the seas for marlin the next.

His work is illustrated with paintings, especially commissioned for this book, by Kevin R. Brant, a fast-rising artist who also has spent many a year on the Florida waters building a firsthand relationship with the characters he paints.

The result is a long-awaited reference book you'll use for all your fishing days.